ANCIENT CLEVELAND
From The Air

ANCIENT CLEVELAND
From The Air

Richard Crosthwaite
M.A. (Cantab)., F.R.S.A., A.R.I.N.A., J.P., D.L.

Published by Tees Towing Co. Ltd.
Middlesbrough

CONTENTS

AERIAL PHOTOGRAPHS

Jacket Illustration

Front — Scarborough

Castle Cliff is a magnificent natural fortress occupied by Bronze Age man, Romans, Anglo-Saxons and Normans. All of these have left their mark on the landscape.

Back — Helmsley

The mediaeval castle built by Robert de Róos in the 12th Century.

Frontispiece

Gemini Sprint Microlight

The photographs in this book were taken from this microlight. Its low speed, unimpeded visibility and modest running costs make it an excellent aircraft for aerial photography. It was flown — and these pictures were taken — by the author.

Opposite Contents

The Cleveland Hills

At 6000ft. (2000m) looking from Nunthorpe towards Roseberry Topping. On the left is Guisborough and on the right is Great Ayton with the geographical fault — known as the whinstone dyke — to its left.

Published by Tees Towing Co., Ltd., Cleveland Buildings, Queens Square, Middlesbrough, Cleveland TS2 1NX, telephone (0642) 247273, from whom copies of this book can be obtained.

ISBN 0 9510232 2 5 Cased

ISBN 0 9510232 3 3 Limp

First Published November 1986
Second Edition June 1987
Third Edition October 1990

Typeset in Times and printed by Lithography by Studio Print, Admiral Chaloner House, Belmangate, Guisborough, Cleveland TS14 7AD, England.

PREFACE

This book is about a corner of England which I have called Ancient Cleveland although the Viking name of Cleveland should — strictly speaking — be applied to the North York Moors only. It covers the area from Durham City to Castle Howard with the eastern edge bounded by the North Sea and western by the A1 (M).

It is an area of the most extraordinary diversity including the highest sea cliffs in England, the lovely Cleveland Hills — fringing industrial Teesside, the lonely moorlands and dales of the North York Moors, and the rich farmlands of the Vales of York and Pickering.

This diversity has always presented a problem for the photographer. The area presents too many facets of countryside and a camera — at ground level — can normally only record one at a time. I have always recognised that aerial photography can overcome this problem but a high winged Cessna and a qualified pilot do not come cheap — so I had to be content with photography from a variety of aircraft flown by a number of long suffering friends.

Then in 1982 hangliders sprouted propellers and I learnt to fly a microlight. The principles of flight are different from other aircraft but the principles of photography are the same, and I was at last able to apply them from an almost perfect aerial platform.

After a few years the local history societies and flying clubs had seen enough of my photographs, and it occurred to me that some of them could be used to to build up a new kind of local history. At first I thought of doing a 'then and now' on the Domesday Book of 1086 but the idea took wing and this book is the result.

The chapters are arranged chronologically with a different map at the beginning of each chapter. Thus in Chapter IV — "THE ROMANS" — the map indicates in red the Roman roads, camps etc., which are mentioned or illustrated in that chapter.

The historical chapters begin by giving the reader some idea of what was going on in the world, while — for instance — our Bronze Age ancestors were building their hillfort on Eston Nab.

All the aerial photographs are listed on pages 6 and 7. They appear in the same order as in the book and are shown with their chapters and page numbers. The index at the back of the book is of course alphabetical.

Those of us who enjoy history feel its charm most vividly when we catch a glimpse of a forgotten way of life in a familiar place. I hope this book will aid that process. Unfortunately it cannot give you all the enjoyment and excitement which its making gave me, but I hope that it may give you an understanding — at a different level — of the magical variety of this corner of England.

Richard Crosthwaite, Great Ayton
Sept. 1986

PRESHISTORIC SITES

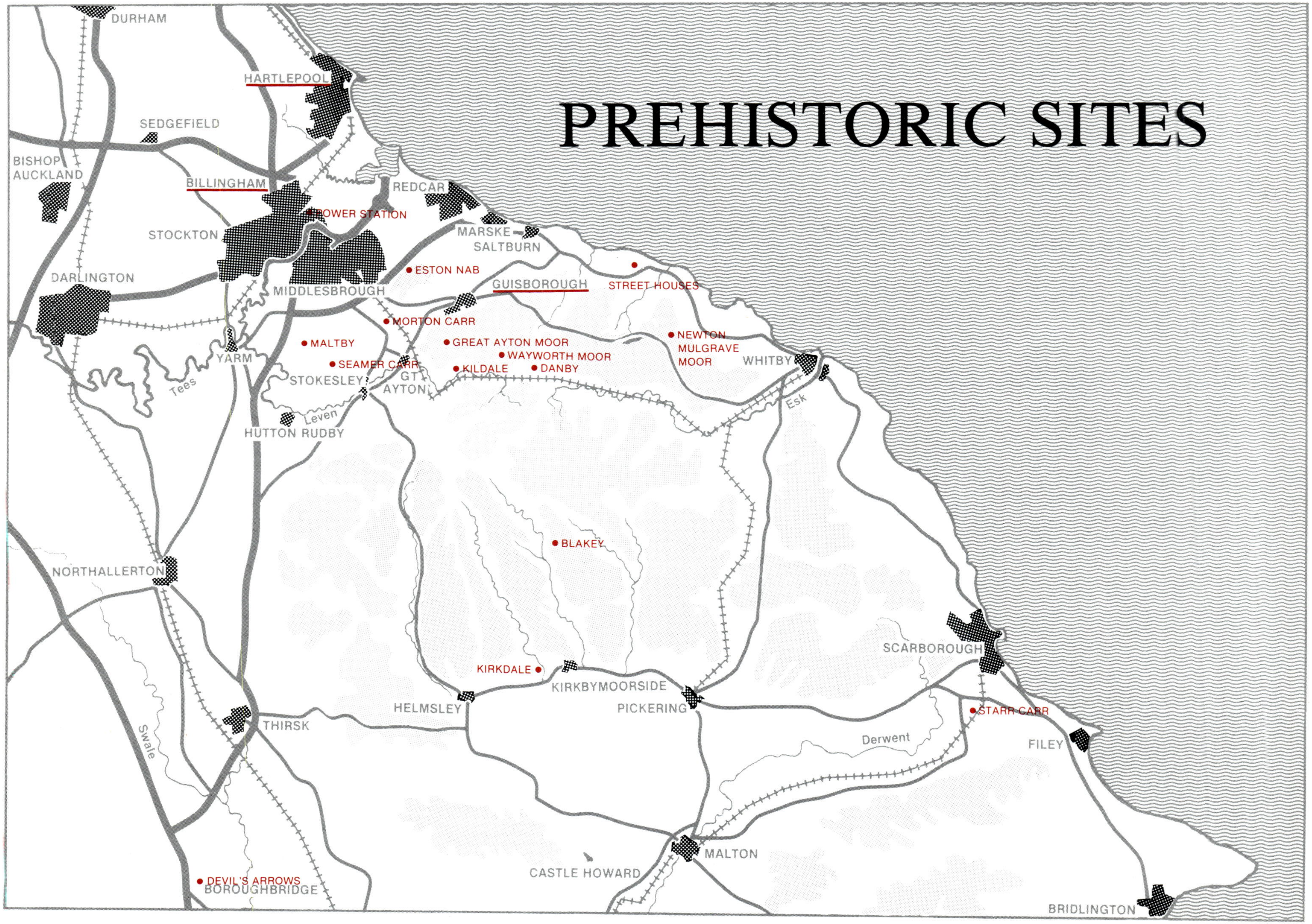

CHAPTER I

PREHISTORIC CLEVELAND

One of the Devil's Arrows, Boroughbridge

Kirkdale, Kirkbymoorside in the Old Stone Age

Earliest Times to 2000 BC

Palaeolithic, Mesolithic and Neolithic Man in Cleveland

Palaeolithic

Throughout the Palaeolithic period all men lived by hunting animals, birds and fish and by gathering wild cereal and vegetables. They used caves for shelter, and no evidence of other types of shelter has survived in this country. Artifacts from the Palaeolithic period other than flints are extremely rare and no artifacts have been found in Cleveland with the possible exception of a flint implement, called an eolith, found on Eston Nab.

"Cup and Ring" Stone found in tumulus near the coast

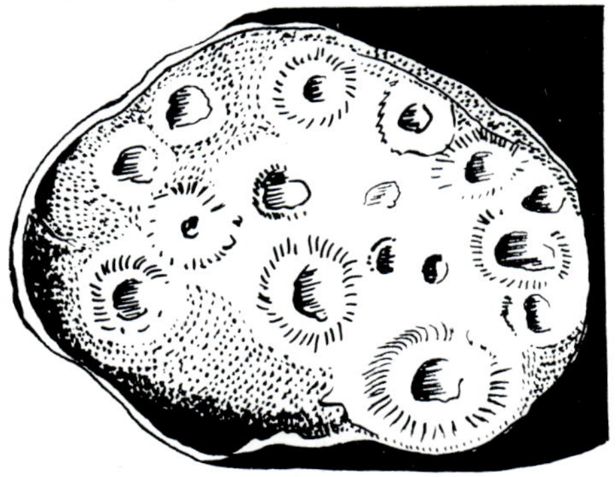

In 1821 bones of a wide variety of prehistoric animals were found in the 'hyena cave' at Kirkdale (Page 13). Dr. Buckland — the Professor of Mineralogy at Oxford University — was confident that these bones belonged to the Palaeolithic period.

The ice age followed the Palaeolithic period and lasted for 500,000 years. During this time the whole of Cleveland, below the level of 800 ft. (260m) was covered with a sheet of ice.

Mesolithic

The glaciers of Cleveland melted about 13,000 BC and left the hilltops surrounded by bare boulder clay. Because the sea level was much lower at that time, the rivers cut very deep channels through the clay and rocks.

The sea rose steadily, due to the ice melting, so that by about 7500 BC the British Isles were cut off from the Continent of Europe. When the Billingham Power Station was being built in 1949 a human skull and animal bones were found 30ft. (10m) below the present sea level and probably date from this period.

In some places the ice melted into natural hollows in the boulder clay and became lakes. These now exist as flat damp depressions known as carrs. Examples of carrs can be found at Morton Carr, Kildale, Seamer Carr and Starr Carr near Filey. As the ice retreated birch and pine forests spread and animals entered the area. During the last century and again in 1975 parts of Seamer Carr were drained and exposed the bones of deer and wild oxen (Page 19). In 1968 the skeleton and large horns of another wild ox were found in the peat bogs near Kildale which were dated at 9400 BC (Page 15). Below these bones a layer of charcoal was found and this probably indicates the first known presence of man in Cleveland.

At Starr Carr in the 1940's a Mesolithic settlement — which may have been an autumn and winter camp — was found. The remains were dated at 8500 BC.

Neolithic

Towards the end of this period the first pharonic dynasty was established in Egypt by King Namer whose exquisite victory palette was carved from slate in 3500 BC. In western Iran some of the most attractive painted pottery ever known was being made and in China the Yang-Shao style of funerary jars achieved a marvellous dynamism.

In the British Isles the first men started pastoral farming in about 3700 BC and are called Neolithic man.

Not a single dwelling of these farmers has been discovered in Cleveland but their burials have been found in stone cairns on Great Ayton Moor and beneath a Bronze Age barrow at Street Houses near Loftus.

The Hyena Cave at Kirkdale

This quiet dale near Kirkbymoorside would not be given more than a glance by most people. They would only see an old church close to a stream with a steep limestone cliff on the far side of the stream. But in this cliff face lies an old quarry in which there are two openings — neither of them more than 3ft. (1m) high — which lead to a considerable cave.

In 1821 bones from this cave were brought to the attention of Dr. William Buckland — Professor of Mineralogy at Oxford. He found most of them to be the bones of between 200 and 300 hyenas. In addition he identified the bones of cave lions, the long extinct great bear, rhinoceros, straight tusked elephants, tigers, wolves, horses, mammoths, bison, Irish elk, red deer, reindeer, wild boar and the extinct giant ox.

At the time those who disputed Darwin's theory of evolution said that the bones proved the literal truth of the great biblical flood. By no other means they said, could the bones of animals from all over the world have arrived in one place unless they had been washed there in a great flood.

However Dr. Buckland was in no doubt that these bones came from the Old Stone Age — the period of history between the last two Ice Ages.

The Neolithic Period lasted until about 2000 BC. Flints and polished axes from this period have been found in the Tees Valley and along the edges of the moors.

Standing stones are common on the North York Moors but cannot usually be dated. The 'Long Stone' near Danby and the 7ft. (2m) stone near Blakey appear to be particularly old and may come from the end of the Neolithic period. None of these stones are as impressive as the Devil's Arrows near Boroughbridge (Page 18). These three enormous blocks of millstone grit must have had a purpose but archaeologists cannot agree on what this was.

The 16 upright stones making up the circle on Wayworth Moor above Commondale (Page 17) belongs to the same Neolithic period as the famous circles of Stonehenge and Avebury in Wiltshire. There can be little doubt that these circles were used as religious temples. Similar circles can be seen in Brittany but Britain and Ireland have most of the examples of this type of megalith.

Kildale
The Arrival of Man

Cleveland emerged from the last ice age in about 13,000 BC. The ice which was up to 800ft. (260m) thick, melted and formed a lake stretching from Kildale to Lealholm.

As the ice retreated the birch and pine forests spread and animals such as the red deer, roe deer, elk, wild oxen and wild boar entered the area.

The remains of some of these animals have been discovered in the peat bogs of Kildale, at the top of the photograph. In 1968 the skeleton of a wild ox with large horns was found at Kildale Hall — top right. The skeleton was dated at 9400 BC and the red deer and reindeer found in the peat bogs during the last century probably came from the same period.

At the same level as the ox a layer of charcoal was found. It seems likely that this charcoal was the first indication of human activity found in the area, although similar traces have been found at other prehistoric swamps at both Seamer Carr near Stokesley and Starr Carr near Filey.

Wayworth Stone Circle

This is the best of the stone circles to be found on the North York Moors. It lies on Wayworth Moor 1½ miles west of Commondale.

The circle consists of 16 upright stones up to 3ft. (1m) above ground level. It is about 60ft (20m) in diameter and has a tumulus on its circumference at 230° (approx. south west), which may have been an altar platform and is in line with Kildale two miles away.

The sheep — which are partly within the circle — indicate that this is not an impressive circle by the standards of Avebury, but there is every reason to suppose that it was constructed for much the same reason — that is — an outdoor temple for late Neolithic man.

The small stones — piled up on the left of the cairn — have recently been collected from the area and help to emphasise the circle. They also provide a source of support for the rather insecure 'megaliths'.

The Devil's Arrows

There are three of these great monoliths of millstone grit standing between Boroughbridge and the A1(M). The road can be seen in the top right hand corner of the photograph and two of the monoliths can be seen from it. The third is in shadow in the drive of the house.

Each stone is about 16ft. (5m) high and was probably transported and erected in much the same way as the inner stones at Stonehenge. In this case they were probably dragged 7 miles from Abbey Plain near Knaresborough.

There are many stone circles in Britain and most archaeologists agree that they were used for religious purposes. However — lines of stones — like the Devil's Arrows are far less common and archaeologists can only agree to disagree about their purpose.

Leland — the 16thC historian — wrote that there was a fourth stone but it was later recorded elsewhere that this stone was lying on the ground and being broken up to be used as building stone for 'Peggy's Bridge' nearby.

Seamer Carr

The photograph shows the village of Seamer near Stokesley. Beyond the village the farmland lies below the 250ft. (80m) contour and contains many drainage ditches and channels.

Low lying areas like these are known as carrs, a term which indicates a peaty area which was once a natural lake or marsh during the Mesolithic period following the melting of the glaciers. We know that this particular carr was marshy — and of no use to farmers — until it was reclaimed in 1815.

Seamer Carr has much in common with Starr Carr near Scarborough and very early evidence of human occupation has been found at the edge of both carrs. Triangular flints blunted on two sides have been found on both sites and so have deer skulls and animal bones with one end pointed and the other formed into a round chisel. Pollen analysis at the level of the finds at Seamer Carr indicated a date of 11,000 BC.

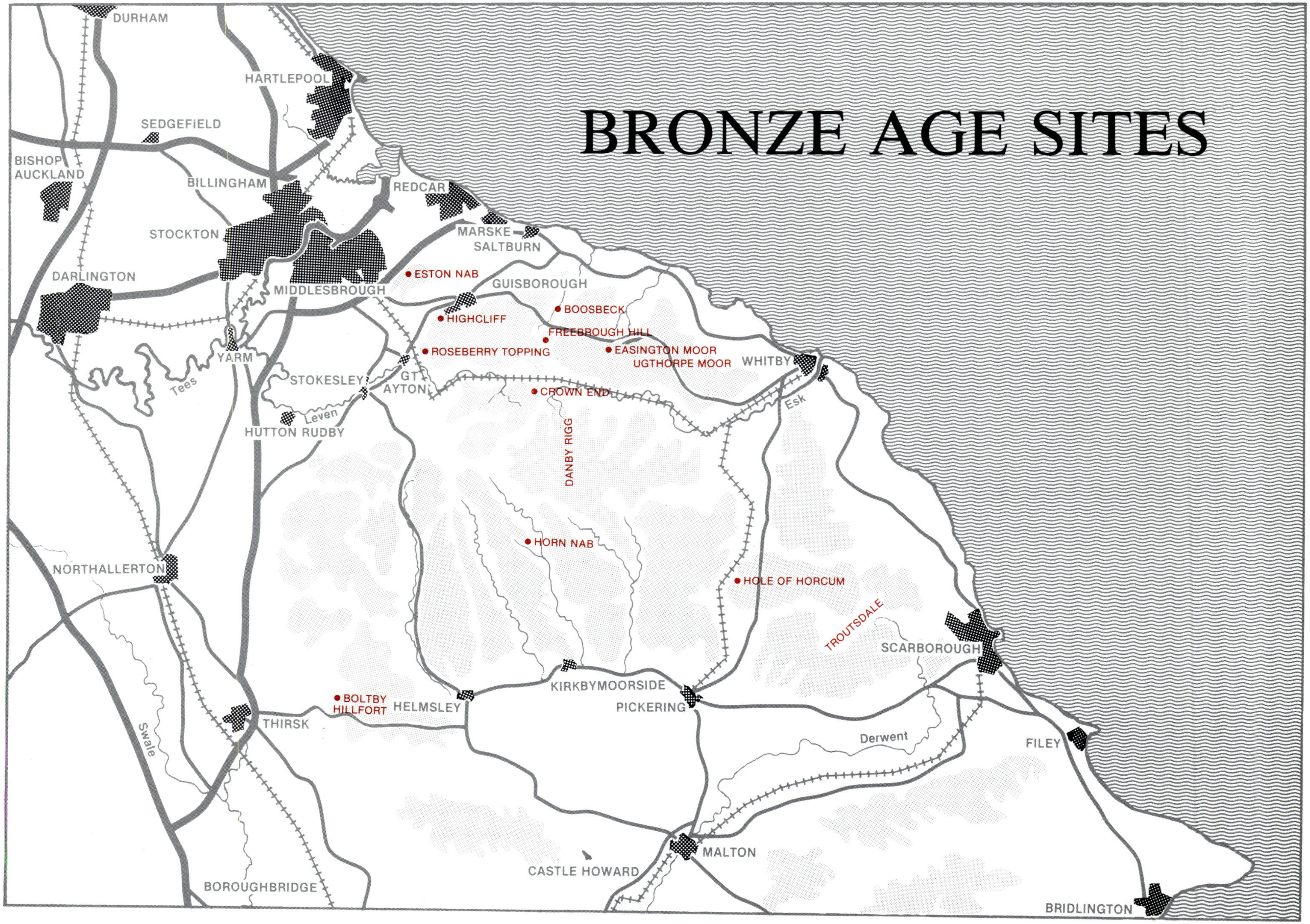
BRONZE AGE SITES
DURHAM
HARTLEPOOL
SEDGEFIELD
BISHOP AUCKLAND
BILLINGHAM
REDCAR
STOCKTON
MARSKE
SALTBURN
DARLINGTON
MIDDLESBROUGH
ESTON NAB
GUISBOROUGH
BOOSBECK
HIGHCLIFF
FREEBROUGH HILL
ROSEBERRY TOPPING
EASINGTON MOOR
UGTHORPE MOOR
WHITBY
YARM
Tees
STOKESLEY
GT AYTON
CROWN END
Esk
Leven
HUTTON RUDBY
DANBY RIGG
HORN NAB
HOLE OF HORCUM
NORTHALLERTON
TROUTSDALE
SCARBOROUGH
KIRKBYMOORSIDE
BOLTBY HILLFORT
HELMSLEY
PICKERING
THIRSK
Swale
Derwent
FILEY
MALTON
CASTLE HOWARD
BOROUGHBRIDGE
BRIDLINGTON

CHAPTER II

Prehistoric	Bronze Age	Iron Age	Romans	Danes	Middle Ages	Modern

THE BRONZE AGE MEN ON THE HILLTOPS

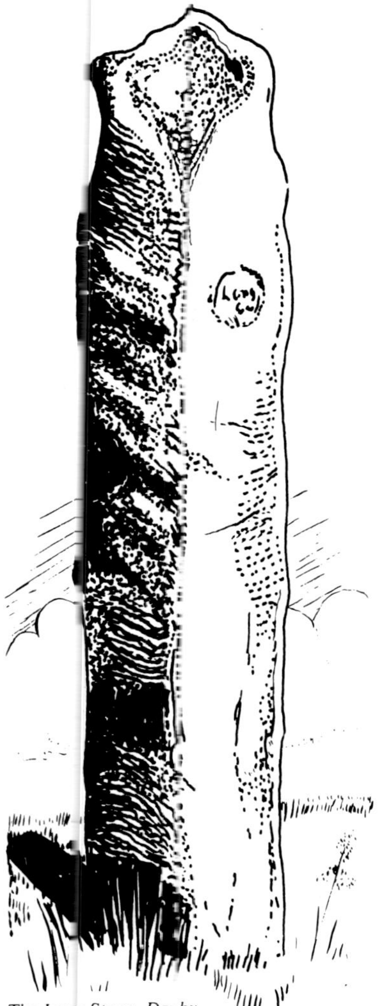

The Long Stone, Darby

Bronze Age farmers outside their enclosure on Eston Nab

2000 BC to 800 BC

At the beginning of the period Egypt was building pyramids and the Sumerians were developing cuniform hieroglyphics but by the end of it the civilisations of the eastern Mediterranean, Egypt and China had flowered. The palace at Knossos in Crete, Solomon's Temple in Jerusalem and the Lion Gate at Mycenae had been built. In Egypt in the Valley of the Kings artists had fashioned the bust of Nefertiti and the Mask of Tutankhamun and in China the Emperors of the Shang dynasty had commissioned the superb bronze ritual vessels which are admired to this day.

Urns found on Guisborough Moor

In Europe it was a period for impressive megalithic tombs and for the outer circles of Stonehenge. Bronze and copper tools were made and used in the British Isles and these must have made a difference to the life of the farmer.

In Cleveland trees were still felled by ring barking and burning rather than with bronze axes, but a magnificent slashing sword was found in the Tees in 1887 and early flanged axes have been found at Boosbeck. In the 1830's a bronze hoard was discovered on Roseberry Topping (Page 154) and it is thought that this was abandoned by a bronze smith some 3000 years ago.

In spite of such findings bronze was undoubtedly a rare metal which was mostly used for prestige activities and the acid soil of Cleveland has ensured that very little of this metal has survived.

Enclosures

The farmers of this period cultivated large areas of the hills above 800ft. (260m) but none of their dwellings in the north-east of England have been identified. This is probably because they were made of wood which, at that time, was still in plentiful supply. However the enclosures which they constructed to protect their dwellings and livestock can still be seen at Wheatbeck above Osmotherley, Near Moor above Swainby, Danby Rigg (Page 27) and at Crown End (Page 29) near Castleton.

Barrows

The main contributions made by Bronze Age people to the Cleveland Hills were their circular burial mounds — known locally as howes. The hills can be seen as an open air museum of the Bronze Age which was first made known by Dr. Elgee in his book "Early Man in North East Yorkshire" published in 1928. The hills and the moors are studded with barrows and cairns constructed in this period, and few areas of Britain can compare with their quantity and variety.

The barrows have suffered over the ages from the plunderings of local people, the zeal of Victorian antiquarians and the persistent activities of ploughmen. However excavations have established two phases of barrow building distinguished by the two types of pottery found in them. The first barrows contained beakers and food vessels and Dr. Elgee found that these were sometimes associated with bronze awls, knives, daggers and axes. The beakers were hand made and may have been used for holding offerings to the dead, (Page 21). They ranged in height from 2″ to 10″ (50mm to 250mm). The second phase of barrows contained larger hand made urns which were sometimes found with 'pygmy cups': small urns which may once have contained incense.

Bronze Age Hillfort Eston Nab

Passed everyday, but rarely noticed by thousands of Teessiders, this hillfort overlooks the Cleveland Parkway and the mining village of Eston.

We cannot even speculate about the dangers which caused early man to build this fort, but between 3000 and 4000 years ago the people living in the Eston Hills dug a large semi-circular ditch on the edge of the sandstone cliff at Eston Nab. It overlooked the sea, the river Tees and a vast marshy estuary which we would not recognise today.

The Rev. Graves first surveyed the site in 1808 but the earliest parts of the fort have not been dated with any certainty. The rampart which is an earthen bank — currently 6ft. (2m) high — is backed by a stone wall which may have carried either a stone or wooden palisade. A small amount of coarse pottery was found beneath the rampart in 1928, and in 1966 some late Bronze Age pottery was found inside the rampart.

Mesolithic flints indicate that the site was used by man from even earlier times. The column inside the fort was built in 1956 from the remains of a beacon tower put up to give warning of a Napoleonic invasion.

Hillforts

The remains of various types of pottery from this period were found inside the hillfort at Eston Nab in 1906 (Page 23). There are similar types of pottery at the Bronze Age fort at Boltby Hill, (now ploughed out). It is not known what dangers caused Bronze Age man to build these forts.

Pit Avenues

These strange lines of pits have been found on Ugthorpe Moor, Danby Rigg, at Troutsdale near Goathland, the Hole of Horcum and on Easington Moor near Scaling Dam (Page 28). This last line of pits was colourfully described by Canon Atkinson in 1881 as a 'British Village' and expeditions to see the pits became popular in Victorian times. Modern archeologists cannot agree on an explanation for these pits and they may have been dug in another period.

Freebrough Hill

Most people travelling on the Guisborough to Whitby Road have wondered about this strangely symmetrical hill. Many assume it to be man-made, like Silbury Hill in Wiltshire. The Victorians felt the same and signs of excavations can be seen just below the summit. However, geologists have shown that Freebrough Hill is entirely natural, its stratas of rock and boulder clay are the same as the surrounding countryside. But striking hills like this — and Roseberry Topping — had a profound effect on prehistoric man and such places often became focal points for their rituals.

The moorland all around the hill is marked with the remains of Bronze Age man. Mounds, groups of barrows, an enclosure and a wide assortment of other earthworks, whose purpose we do not fully understand, were constructed in this area. The site looks towards the sea and was on the high ground well above the marshes of 2000 BC.

Much later, when the Romans had left Britain, the Anglo-Saxons made Cleveland a part of their northern kingdom of Deira. These people worshipped Freya — their goddess of fertility and named the hill after her.

Bronze Axe Head from Roseberry Topping

Danby Rigg

None of the interesting archaeological terrains of the north east have such a striking — almost chilling — effect on the flier than Danby Rigg. After the friendly green dales of Eskdale, Danby Dale and Little Fryup Dale the forbidding black mass of the rigg seems an unlikely home for Bronze Age man.

Frank Elgee was responsible for the first survey of this area. He found that it had one of the greatest concentrations of cairns to be found in the British Isles and had no hesitation in referring to the north end of the rigg as a cemetery. He was the first to record the Double Dykes, and described them as 'two ramparts separated by a deep foss at the east end; three ramparts with two intervening fosses at the west end'. Some of these dykes can be seen in the photograph just above the 'waist' of the rigg. In the area between the two cross ridges Elgee found a burial mound — 70ft (25m) in diameter — enclosing a central grave. He also found an enclosure, some field systems, cairns and pits.

Until Danby Rigg can be properly excavated we can only conclude that it must have been a site which was inhabited by Bronze Age man for a considerable period of time. But the area is so devastated that it seems unlikely that any clear conclusions will ever be drawn about its purpose.

The Pits on Easington Moor

These remarkable avenues of pits have defied archaeological explanation for over 100 years. The pits are almost 3ft. (1m) deep and 7ft. (2m) across and form a double line just south of Scaling Dam. There are other lines running from behind Roseberry Topping to Highcliff near Guisborough, in Troutsdale, near Goathland ("the killing pits") and near the Hole of Horcum.

In 1881 the proximity of standing stones and barrows caused Canon Atkinson to describe these pits seen in the photograph as the remains of a British Village and excursions to view them became popular in Victorian times. Later on, archaeologists including Canon Atkinson, decided that no-one would choose to live in water logged pits, so that explanation fell out of favour.

The various sets of pits may have no common origin. In some cases they may have been fossikings for jet or iron. However in 1926 it was shown that the Roseberry pits had nothing to do with mining and may have been military works of an unknown date.

All that archaeologists seem able to agree on is that the pits were constructed between the end of the Bronze Age and the end of the mediaeval period, and may have been some kind of boundary.

Bronze Age Enclosure on Westerdale Moor

This late Bronze Age enclosure is two miles west of Castleton on a spur of Westerdale Moor known as Crown End.

It was first excavated in 1928 by Dr. Elgee who was particularly interested in a number of shallow pits which he found in the area. He thought that these might have been prehistoric storage pits or mediaeval ironstone bell pits.

The earthworks of the enclosure, which can be seen in the foreground of the photograph, probably belong to the Bronze Age period. Beyond the enclosure many hut foundations, barrows, lynchets and clearance cairns, belonging to the same period have been identified. It is thought that the lynchets were each surmounted with stone walls and that these defined the limits of cultivated plots.

The more prominent barrows have been excavated in modern times, but the majority had already had their burial urns removed.

IRON AGE SITES

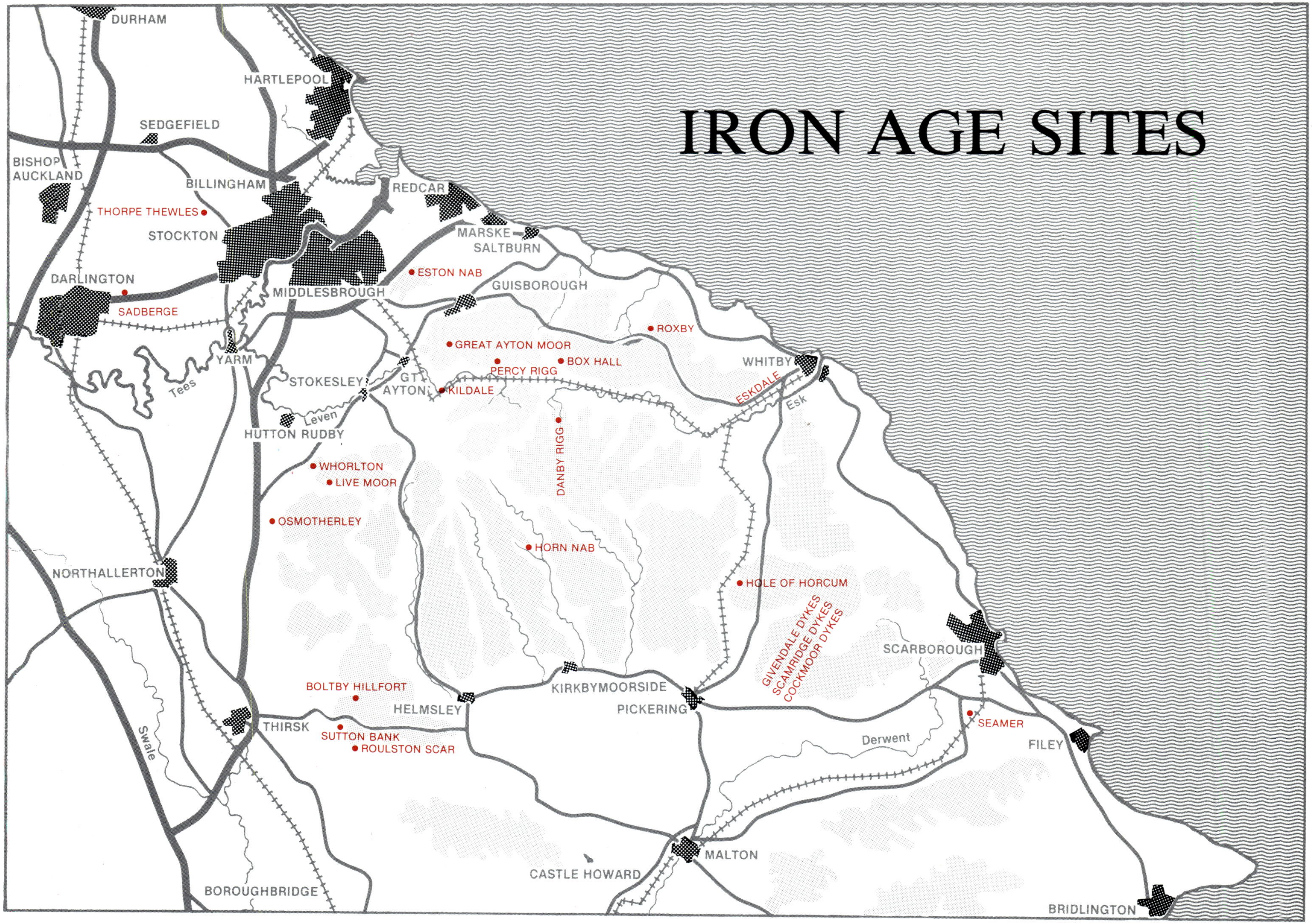

CHAPTER III

Prehistoric	Bronze Age	Iron Age	Romans	Danes	Middle Ages	Modern

THE IRON AGE MEN IN THE FOOTHILLS

800 BC to 71 AD

Iron Age farmers on Great Ayton Moor

Hut from Iron Age settlement — Thorpe Thewles

If the Bronze Age saw the flowering of great civilisations across the world, the Iron Age saw the consolidation of these civilisations and the explosion of Greek thought which was to lead eventually to western civilisation. It was in this period that the Parthenon was built in Athens, that Archimedes developed his screw for raising water and Hero pioneered the steam turbine. In the Far East the Chinese built the Great Wall of China which is the only man-made object which can be seen from the moon.

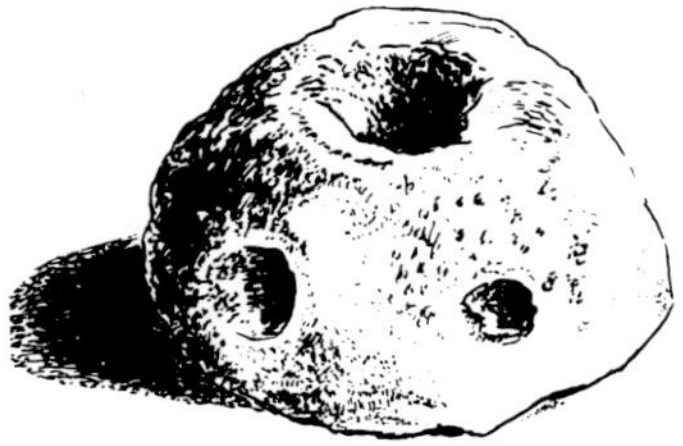

Iron Age quern from Great Ayton Moor

By comparison most of Continental Europe lagged behind. In Denmark 'Tollund men' — now known as the bog people — were still leading a primitive lifestyle, and in the British Isles the most advanced buildings were the inner circles at Stonehenge and the brochs in the Orkneys and Shetlands.

In the Cleveland area, the Iron Age was marked by the emergence of the Celts and a catastrophic deterioration in the climate. The Celts did not erect standing stones and did not bury their dead in barrows as the Bronze Age people had done. The upper parts of the hills above 800 ft. (260m) were abandoned because of the weather and because the light sandy soils had been worked out.

The Celts developed improved methods of bronze casting and, later on, the knowledge of iron smelting helped them to make tools which could work the heavier clay soils below 800 ft. (260m). One of the immediate effects of their movement into the lower parts of the hills was the drastic depredation of the natural forest by slashing and burning. They won their new field systems but the bare appearance of the moors dates from this period.

Many beehive querns — used in grinding corn — have been found on the edges of the North York Moors, notably at sites in Kildale and Eskdale. At Sadberge an iron slashing sword dating from this period was found in 1880 and is now in the British Museum.

Caesar tells us that the Gabrantovices ('horse riding fighters') were a sub-division of the Brigante tribe and lived somewhere in the Cleveland area. These people named the rivers — Tees, Tame, Leven and Esk.

Settlements

The settlements of the Iron Age people fall into two types. The first consists of round-houses which were circular huts with roofs made of turf. Remains of this type can be found at Roxby (Page 38), Percy Rigg above Kildale and Thorpe Thewles.

The second type consists of round-houses which were surrounded by a ditch and bank. This type is known as enclosures and can be seen at Roxby, Great Ayton Moor (Page 33), Box Hall near Castleton and Thorpe Thewles (Page 37).

Hillforts

Juvenal wrote about "the hillforts of the Brigantes" and it is tempting to suggest that these were constructed to repel the Romans. However, the dating of the hillforts in the Cleveland area does not confirm this. Few of these forts have been properly excavated but some have provided evidence of both Bronze Age and Iron Age occupation.

Iron Age Enclosure on Great Ayton Moor

For some reason these conspicuous earthworks were largely ignored by archaeologists until the 1960's.

The site looks south-east towards Lonsdale and south-west to the Iron Age fort above Whorlton.

Pollen analysis of the soil beneath the bank of the enclosure shows that, at the time of construction, the countryside round about was open grassland rather than the bracken and heather which overrun the site today. The arable field system near to the enclosure was probably developed at about the same time.

The enclosure itself consists of a stoney earth bank and ditch with an entrance half way along its left hand side. The foundations of a paved hut — of unusual oval shape — were found within the enclosure. There were no post holes — which would have indicated a wooden palisade — on top of the earthen bank.

Pottery found on the site was dated at 300-100 BC or earlier and indicated occupation into the late Iron Age.

The circular depressions around the enclosure are the remains of Bronze Age burial mounds. The finds from these sites have been deposited in the Dorman Museum, Middlesbrough.

The hillfort at Eston Nab (Page 23) comes in this last category, but there are similar hillforts on Live Moor (Page 39), Horn Nab above Farndale and at both Boltby Hill and Roulston Scar near Sutton Bank.

Dykes

No archaeological remains in the area covered by this book excite so much speculation as the earthen dykes in Bilsdale and in the Scamridge area north of the Pickering to Scarborough road. There are similar — although less dramatic — dykes on the moors south of the Hole of Horcum and above Seamer near Scarborough.

These dykes appear to be different from the defensive dykes of the cross ridge kind found on Danby Rigg (Page 27) and different from the field markers of the Cleave Dyke kind found between Sutton Bank and Osmotherley.

The Scamridge dyke system in the Tabular hills consists of Red Dyke, Wide Dyke, Gibbendale Dyke, Moor Dyke, the Oxmoor Dykes, the Cockmoor Dykes as well as the Scamridge Dyke (Page 35). Many of the dykes in the Scamridge system run for 2 or 3 miles; sometimes they are single and sometimes several run abreast. The Cockmoor Dykes are the most extraordinary of them all with no less than 20 ditches and banks of various sizes. Some of the banks are believed to be mediaeval and may have been constructed for rabbit warrening, but most archaeologists believe that the earliest dykes were elaborate boundary markers.

Scamridge Dyke

The tree line carving its way across the landscape marks Scamridge Dyke — the best known of the Iron Age dykes and the one which has given its name to the system lying to the north of the Pickering road to Scarborough. These vast boundary markers are peculiar to England and their size contradicts the idea that Iron Age man restricted his farming to small clearings in the prehistoric forest.

Part of the triple ditches of the Scamridge Dyke can be seen in the photograph. Most of the dykes are overgrown with trees but these may have helped to prevent ploughing out over the ages.

The size and width of these dykes are imposing enough but the Cockmoor dykes hidden behind the small wood-top right — consist of about 20 ditches and banks of various sizes. Although some of these may have been mediaeval rabbit warrens, eminent archaeologists from Elgee to Mortimer, have failed to produce a convincing explanation for their astonishing complexity.

The Scamridge Dykes cannot be 'kingdom' boundaries as there are too many of them. They make no sense as military boundaries so perhaps they are no more than the Iron Age equivalent of parish boundaries.

Slashing Sword and Scabbard from the Tees

Thorpe Thewles Settlement

In 1977 a light aircraft was flying over farmland near Thorpe Thewles — on the Stockton road to Sedgefield — when the passenger who was an amateur archaeologist noticed that the uneven ripening of barley showed the outline of what looked like an Iron Age enclosure.

Excavations, which began in 1980, confirmed this opinion and revealed an enclosure and complex series of foundations of round-houses. These had been used to shelter farmers and their stock and to store grain.

The excavations were carried out in a systematic manner using modern techniques and this approach made it possible to produce an artist's impression of what the settlement looked like in 100 BC.

There is an exhibtion about this important Iron Age site at Station House in the village of Thorpe Thewles.

ANDREW HUTCHINSON

Roxby Settlement

On each side of the Roxby to Scaling road, running alongside the right hand side of the photograph, are the remains of two Iron Age enclosures and up to about 20 huts which together may be considered the Iron Age predecessor of Roxby village.

One of the enclosures can be seen in the foreground, and at the top of the photograph are circular foundations which probably served a number of specialised purposes. There is another foundation to the right of the crossroads with a number of holloways running up to it.

The remains provide convincing evidence that there was a healthy, although elementary, Iron Age economy in the dales of the Cleveland Hills. Similar settlements like the one on Percy Rigg above Kildale, suggest a co-operative kind of economy which made use of local pottery, bowl iron furnaces and beehive rotary querns.

The fact that these settlements could survive in heavy clay soils suggests that Iron Age man was capable of farming a considerable range of soils.

Hillfort on Live Moor

This ancient hillfort of Knolls End overlooks Wharlton near Swainby, but it was only fourteen years ago that these earthworks on Live Moor were recognised from the air. The track seen running along the left hand side is the Cleveland Way but for years none of the walkers noticed anything unusual.

Because the discovery is recent it is too early to say precisely what kind of purpose the earthworks served. The banks appear to be too high for an Iron Age enclosure and it seems likely that this was an Iron Age hillfort. If this is the case there may have been a wooden palisade on top of the rampart.

Behind the palisade the Celts of the Gabrantovices tribe may have watched the Roman legions marching north along Hambleton Street just 1½ miles in front of them.

ROMAN SITES

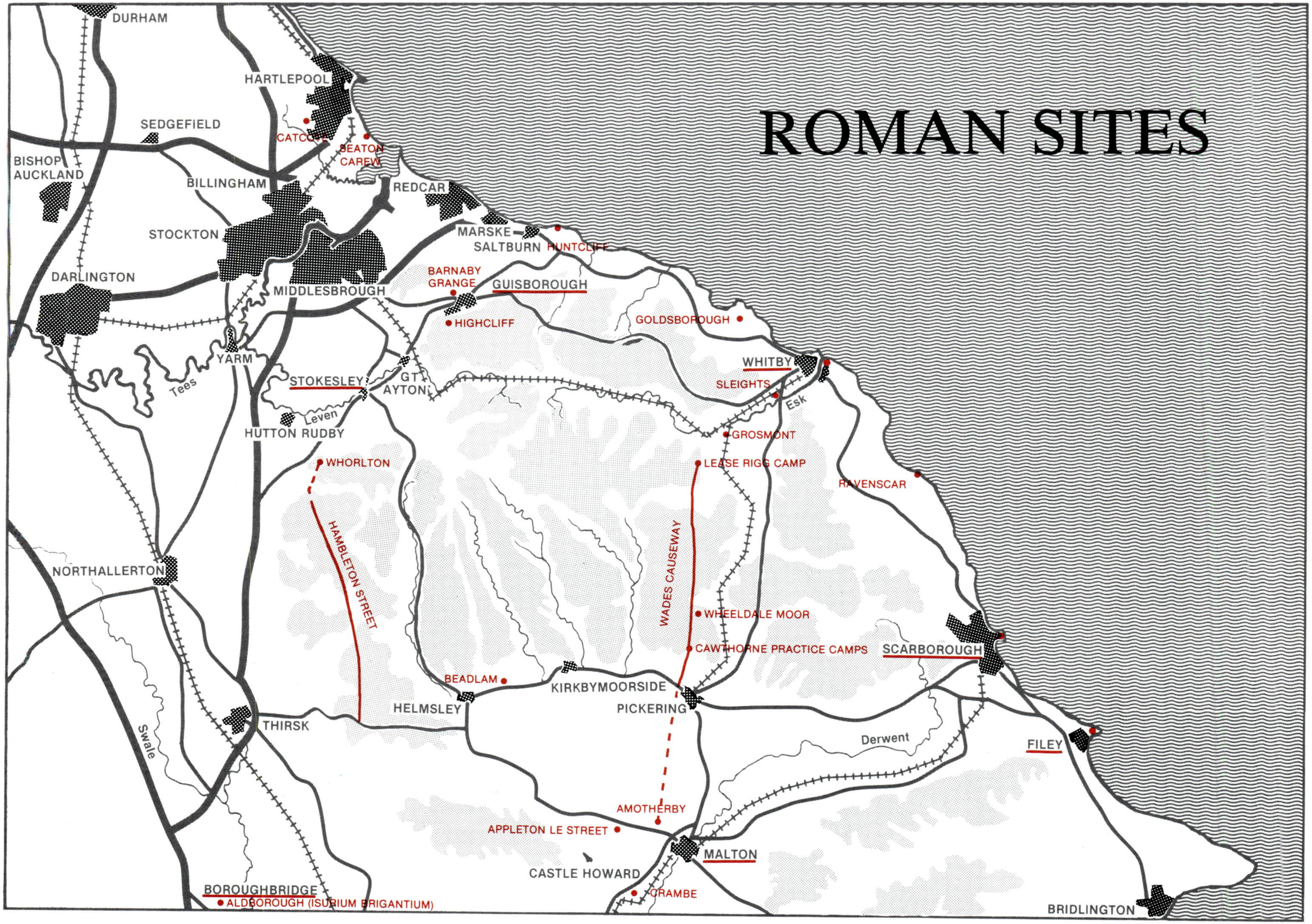

DURHAM
HARTLEPOOL
SEDGEFIELD
CATCOTE
SEATON CAREW
BISHOP AUCKLAND
BILLINGHAM
REDCAR
STOCKTON
MARSKE
SALTBURN
HUNTCLIFF
DARLINGTON
BARNABY GRANGE
GUISBOROUGH
MIDDLESBROUGH
HIGHCLIFF
GOLDSBOROUGH
YARM
WHITBY
GT AYTON
STOKESLEY
SLEIGHTS
Tees
Esk
Leven
HUTTON RUDBY
GROSMONT
WHORLTON
LEASE RIGG CAMP
RAVENSCAR
HAMBLETON STREET
WADES CAUSEWAY
NORTHALLERTON
WHEELDALE MOOR
CAWTHORNE PRACTICE CAMPS
SCARBOROUGH
BEADLAM
KIRKBYMOORSIDE
HELMSLEY
PICKERING
THIRSK
Swale
Derwent
FILEY
AMOTHERBY
APPLETON LE STREET
MALTON
CASTLE HOWARD
BOROUGHBRIDGE
ALDBOROUGH (ISURIUM BRIGANTIUM)
CRAMBE
BRIDLINGTON

THE ROMANS

71 AD to 410 AD

The man who won the Empire

Signal Station on the cliff top at Huntcliff

Inscription from the Signal Station, Ravenscar

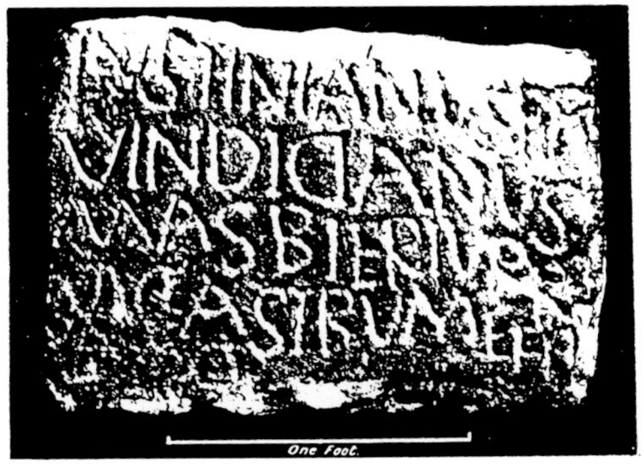

The Roman civilisation was of such incalculable importance to western civilisation that Europeans are inclined to overlook other civilisations.

However, it was in this period that the Hindu and Buddhist religions developed and spread their culture throughout the Far East, and the beautiful Chinese flying horses were cast in bronze by the craftsmen of the Han Empire. In the Andes, the huge Pyramid of the Sun was constructed in Teotihuacan, and Mayan architecture and art emerged in the form of intricate glyphics which enabled the Mayans to record their history.

The countries abutting the Mediterranean were conquered by the Roman armies which relied heavily on the practical inventions of their engineers, many of whom had been educated in Greece. These engineers also developed under-floor heating and assisted the architects in remarkable feats of architecture, such as the Pantheon, whose immense dome depends upon the skilled use of concrete. Greco-Roman art dominated all forms of artistic expressions throughout the Roman Empire and Celtic art declined. Submission to the Roman armies was closely followed by the benefits of Roman civilisation in a period which is known as Romano-British. This period lasted from Claudius' arrival in England in 43 AD until the departure of the Romans.

The mighty hillforts in the south of England — including Maiden Castle in Dorset — soon fell to the Romans and the Celtic leader Caractacus was taken to Rome where he exclaimed "Why do you, with all these great possessions still covet our poor huts?" However, it was not long before the Celtic aristocracy had exchanged their poor huts for fine Romano-British villas.

The best known achievements of Rome in this period are well planned towns such as St. Albans, London, Colchester, Bath and York. Most of these contained a forum, basilica, market hall, theatre, amphitheatre and a number of temples. The buildings were well served with roads, sewers, public baths and fresh water delivered by aquaduct. Aldborough (Page 47), near Boroughbridge is the town, in the area covered by this book, which came nearest to matching these facilities.

Boadicea in East Anglia and the Brigantes in Yorkshire were not as easily defeated as the Celtic tribes in the south and it was not until 71 AD that the XXth Legion from Wroxeter and the IXth Legion from Lincoln, finally subdued the area. The Legion stationed at York was either the VIth (Spanish) or the IXth and the military position in the north of England was consolidated with the completion of Hadrian's Wall in about 130 AD. By that time, Agricola had installed garrisons in a number of centres and had laid out a strategic road network.

Roman Signal Station Huntcliff

Huntcliff is 365ft. (120m) above sea level and is one of the highest cliffs in England. It was the site chosen by the Romans for their coastguard signal station built to warn against invading Pict and Saxon ships.

The station had a well and walls which were 5ft. (1.5m) thick. It was probably constructed by Theodosius in the second half of the fourth century.

Smoke by day and fire by night was the signal which was relayed to the garrisons at Malton, Catterick and Piercebridge. Remains of what may have been the first relay station, have been discovered near Highcliff above Guisborough.

Thanks to the excavations of 1911 we know quite a lot about the fate of this coastguard station. Some time around 390 AD a band of fourteen who had been living in some squalor in the station, were caught unawares by a raiding party which must have landed on the beach below. All fourteen were hit on the head and their bodies thrown into the well. Many of the artifacts from this well can be seen in Whitby Museum.

The station, its well and defences have now fallen into the sea and the photograph shows the under cutting effect of the waves. There is a commemorative plaque on the edge of the cliff.

Military Roads and Camps

In the Cleveland area the most important of these roads is now known as Wade's Causeway. This was a military road running from York, by-passing Malton, skirting Appleton-le-Street and leading to the very striking practice camps at Cawthorne (Page 45). The road then continued north to the marching camp at Lease Rigg near Grosmont, and may have gone on to serve the coastal signal stations. The best preserved part of this road can be seen near Wheeldale Lodge (Page 49).

Roman Sites

Farm Villas have been excavated at Beadlam, Sleights, and Newbiggin Hall and some remarkable finds, not associated with these villas, have been found in other parts of the area. In 1864 a gilded brass parade helmet — much mutilated and dated to the late 3rdC — was found at Barnaby Grange west of Guisborough and a 4thC pewter jug was discovered when Eller Beck was being re-directed round Stokesley. Throughout the area many deposits of 4thC pottery — originally from Crambe near Castle Howard — have been found.

More substantial sites of Roman occupation have been found at Whorlton (Page 50), Seaton Carew and Catcote near West Hartlepool. It was at such sites that a shortage of 2ndC pottery and coins was noticed and this coincides with the time of the Brigante revolt.

Coastguard Stations

In order to give warning of seaborne attacks in the latter part of the 4thC, small stone forts were built at Huntcliff (Page 43), Goldsborough (Page 51), Ravenscar and Scarborough and there might have been others at Hartlepool, Whitby and Filey. These were built as a direct result of the seaborne attacks of 367 AD when Hadrian's Wall was outflanked. All of these forts were built to a similar design with a stone curtain wall enclosing a central tower of at least two storeys.

In 406 AD Gaul was overrun by tribes from across the Rhine and Britain was cut off from the Empire. In 410 AD the British cities wrote to the Emperor Honorius asking for help but he replied that he could not help and that they must look to their own defence. About this time Hadrian's Wall was abandoned but as late as 429 AD there are records suggesting that the towns still maintained a semblance of law and order even though the countryside was in chaos.

Very shortly afterwards the shutters came down and recorded history in the Cleveland area came to an end: the Dark Ages had begun.

Cawthorne Practice Camps

The four Roman camps at Cawthorne near Pickering, are unlike any camps found in Continental Europe. They occupy 36 acres — and being in an unusually fine state of preservation — have been scheduled as Ancient Monuments.

For many years the overlapping nature of the camps presented a mystery and little was known other than the fact that their date of construction was about 100 AD.

However in the 1920's and 30's Professor Sir Ian Richmond undertook a series of major excavations from which he concluded that the area was occupied on two separate occasions each time by legionaries who lived in one camp and built another. The fact that the site was unsuitable for permanent occupation, and that two of the camps had been abandoned before they were finished, forced him to the conclusion that the legionaries had been on manoeuvres and not involved in active warfare. In short the earthworks had been practice camps.

Unfortunately the well preserved appearance of the camps from the air has been deteriorating since 1945 when a period of natural re-generation of the woodland began. The craters made by mortar practice in World II have been obscured.

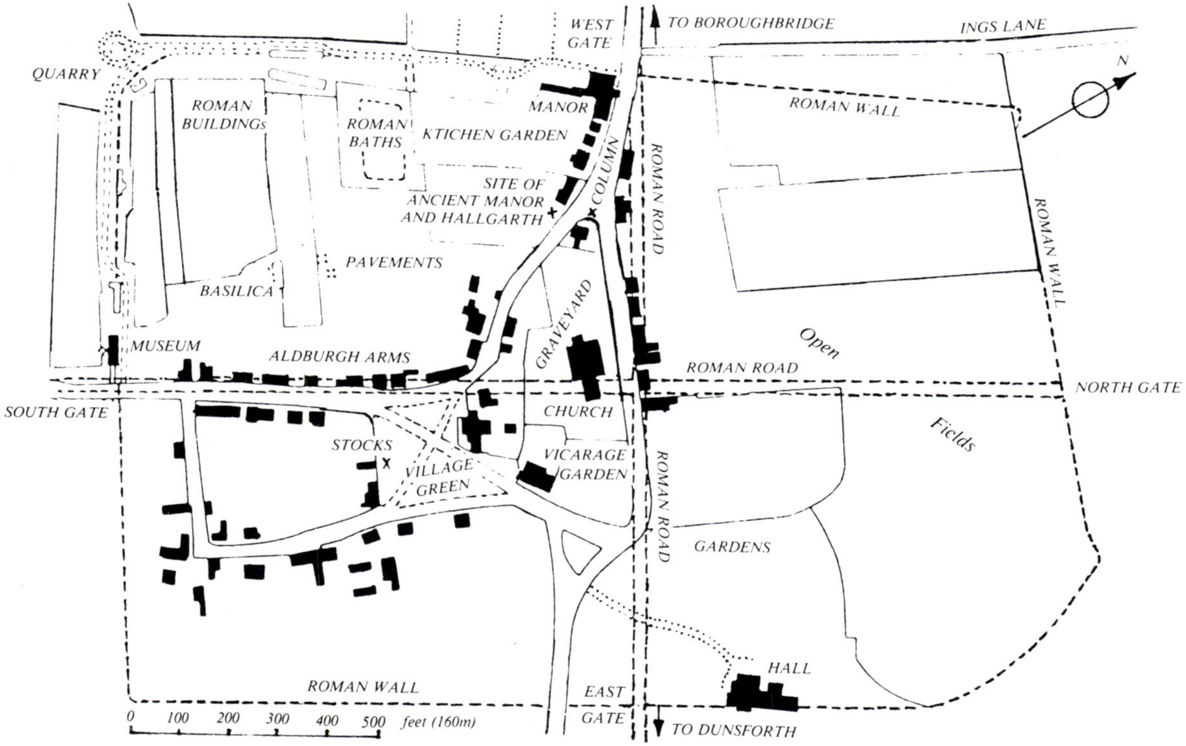

ALDBOROUGH

Aldborough — Isurium Brigantium

This Roman town is potentially one of the most important archaeological sites in Britain but a full scale excavation is unlikely to take place unless the town is threatened by a major re-development.

The ford across the River Ure determined its site. The Romans transported great quantities of corn from Lincolnshire along the Ouse and the Ure to the wharf at Hall Arm which lies ¼ mile to the right of the photograph.

The plan of Isurium followed the usual pattern of a Roman town which was a rectangle covering about 55 acres. York at the same time covered 50 acres. The positions of the principal Roman structures such as the walls, baths, basilica and gates can be found by comparing the photograph with the plan on the left.

By 74 AD the Brigantes in the north had been subdued by Agricola and Petilius Cerialis — the son of the Emperor Vespasian. The town became one of the fourteen cantonal capitals in Britian but the defences were not completed until about 150 AD. These defences must have presented a formidable sight as they consisted of huge walls of red sandstone with a high bank and watch towers behind the walls.

The town declined when the Romans built a bridge over the Ure at Boroughbridge. The Anglo-Saxons valued its position as much as the Romano-British. They named it Burc and it flourished as a regional capital until the Danes burnt it to the ground in 870 AD.

The Scarborough Signal Station

Of all the signal stations which the Romans built along our coast line, this is the only one whose remains can still be seen.

The other stations at Huntcliff, Goldsborough and Ravenscar were built to a similar plan in about 370 AD. All of them had a high square beacon tower standing in the centre of a square courtyard surrounded by a high wall. This courtyard led to an outer courtyard on the land side and the whole station was protected by a deep ditch. All this can be seen in the photograph except the east wall and ditch which have fallen into the sea.

The ditch on the north side is obscured by a mediaeval well known as Our Lady's Well built about the year 1000 AD and thought to be miraculous because the water lay within 10ft (3m) of the surface of the cliff top. The wall of the chapel, which was built over the well, was once part of the wall of the signal station and was probably destroyed when Harold Hardradra King of Norway invaded Yorkshire in 1066, and thereby paved the way for the Norman victory a few days later.

The remains of later chapels may lie beneath the earthworks seen at the bottom of the photograph but these have still to be excavated. We do know however that it was in this area that Bronze Age men from the Rhineland built a settlement 800 years before the Romans arrived. One of their jet rings can be seen in the town's Rotunda Museum.

Roman Road in Wheeldale

There seems little difference between the two roads in the photograph, but the one on the left is modern and the one on the right is almost 2000 years old.

When the IXth and XXth legions were sent to subdue the Brigantes in 71 AD they built a road from Amotherby near Malton, which skirted Appleton-le-Street, and continued to the Cawthorne Camps near Pickering where it was to become known as Wade's Causeway. It continued north through Wheeldale, along Lease Rigg to the camp there and on to Grosmont.

The road shown formed part of Agricola's military network in the north of England although it seems certain that it was also used for the carriage of civilian goods — including jet which was highly prized in the Roman Empire.

This well preserved stretch of road is shown at the point where it passes over Wheeldale Moor. It then descended into the dale and crossed Wheeldale Beck via a wooden bridge whose stone supports have been identified. Like many Roman roads it was constructed of stone blocks held in position by kerbs and usually laid on a base of rammed clay. It had a camber and side ditches, and milestones were placed along it. These stones were cylindrical in shape and inscribed with the relevant distances and the name of the Emperor.

Contrary to popular opinion the photograph shows that not all Roman roads ran as straight as a die!

Whorlton Camp

Whorlton means "the homestead on the hill shaped like a whorl". The Iron Age fort shown on Page 39 looks down on Whorlton, and Celtic Warriors of the Gabrantovices tribe may have watched the Roman legions advance along what was to become Hambleton Street — and construct their marching camp on the flanks of the hill.

The marching camp at Lease Rigg on Wade's Causeway is the only Roman camp in the area which has been verified by excavation. However authorities since Victorian times have been aware of the earthworks shown in the photograph and have pointed out that the dimensions of the banks and ditches, and the shape of the break on the near side, conform to what would be expected in a Roman camp.

More than a thousand years after the Romans left, the Lord of the Manor of Whorlton constructed a deer park. Only excavation will be able to establish whether these earthworks were built to keep deer in or Celts out.

Signal Station at Goldsborough

The remains of this signal station lie half a mile inland at a height of 425ft. (140m) which is higher than the Huntcliff Station, but in a less dramatic situation.

After the excavations between 1918 and 1923 the remains of the station were covered over, but the site can be seen on the photograph mid way between Goldsborough village and the Kettleness alum mine — which was the last of its kind to close in England.

The excavations showed that — apart from Scarborough — this was the best preserved of the signal stations on the east coast. The outer wall was found to be 4ft (1.5m) thick at the base and protected by a defensive ditch 12ft (4m) wide. The remains of a well and oven were also found. The square stone tower must have been similar to the one at Huntcliff. There is a complete reconstruction in model form to be seen in Whitby Museum.

The excavations uncovered some interesting artifacts including pottery, bronze bracelets, rings, Romano-British cloth, jet ornaments and kitchen bowls which show the incorporation of grit in the bottom of the bowl.

The skulls of five adults including two men who had died sudden deaths inside the tower, were found. It seems possible that this station was overcome by Anglo-Saxon raiders early in the 5thC AD.

ANGLO SAXON & VIKING SITES
DURHAM
HART
HARTLEPOOL
SEDGEFIELD
BISHOP AUCKLAND
BILLINGHAM
REDCAR
NORTON
STOCKTON
MARSKE
HOB HILL
SALTBURN
NORMANBY
DARLINGTON
MIDDLESBROUGH
ORMESBY
GUISBOROUGH
TOLLESBY
STAINTON
HILTON
GOLDSBOROUGH
YARM
WHITBY
GT. AYTON
STOKESLEY
KILDALE
DANBY
Tees
SOCKBURN
Leven
INGLEBY GREENHOW
Esk
HUTTON RUDBY
INGLEBY ARNCLIFFE
BROMPTON
NORTHALLERTON
LASTINGHAM
SCARBOROUGH
MIDDLETON
KIRKDALE
KIRKBYMOORSIDE
HELMSLEY
PICKERING
THIRSK
Derwent
FILEY
Swale
HOVINGHAM
MALTON
CASTLE HOWARD
BOROUGHBRIDGE
BRIDLINGTON

CHAPTER V

Prehistoric	Bronze Age	Iron Age	Romans	Danes	Middle Ages	Modern

THE DANISH CONNECTION

410 AD to 1066

10thC Cross with Viking at Middleton

Anglo-Saxons at Hob Hill with Huntcliff in the background

The Gokstad Ship whose replica sailed the Atlantic in 1893

The decline and fall of the Roman Empire in Cleveland marked the end of civilisation for more than six hundred years.

In Europe, law and order collapsed under the onslaught of the barbarians beyond the Rhine and what little learning remained was only to be found in Benedictine monasteries and in Charlemagne's short-lived attempt to restore the old values in the Holy Roman Empire. Mohammed was born in 570 AD and by the time of his death the Islamic Empire stretched from North Africa to the borders of India. In Europe its spread was only halted by the Franks at Tours in 732 AD after Spain and northern Italy had already fallen. It was a close thing for Christianity!

In Asia, Hinduism continued to expand and Buddhism was introduced into Japan. In China, the T'ang Dynasty was enjoying its golden age and in the Americas, the Toltecs had learnt how to smelt metal and had built an empire in the valley of Mexico.

In England "Anglo-Saxon" was to become the convenient label for the whole period from the departure of the Romans to the Norman Conquest. The first raiders were Saxons from Germany and these settled in the Thames valley and Wessex. After them, Jutes from northern Denmark and Frisians from northern Holland settled in the Isle of Wight and in Kent where they clashed with Franks from France and Belgium. In the south-west of England, the flame of civilisation and Christianity was, for a time, kept alight by groups of Romano-British, whose courageous rearguard actions were to be immortalised in the Arthurian legends.

In the north-east of England, the first raiders and settlers were Angles who came from Denmark and Schleswig-Holstein. By the 7thC they had formed the Kingdom of Northumbria, but the part south of the Tees soon split off and became Deira. It was from Deira that the Anglian slaves — seen in Rome by Pope Gregory the Great — came. "These are not Angles but angels" he is said to have exclaimed and St. Augustine was despatched to England, where he converted the Saxon king of Kent.

Early in the 9thC the Vikings began raiding the coast of Cleveland and they too came from Denmark. Of these Danes, the Venerable Bede lamented "The Barbarians drive us into the sea and the sea drives us back to the Barbarians. Between these, two deadly alternatives confront us — drowning or slaughter". It was the Vikings who gave the name Cleveland — "the land of cliffs" — to the area which stretched from the Tees to Scarborough and much of which was to become the wapentake of Langbaurgh.

The Angles and the Vikings built their houses of wood and there is no archaeological evidence in Cleveland of substantial settlements or trading centres of the kind found in York. The Angles are thought to have used acre fields of 220 yds x 20 yds, but there is no evidence of these, nor of the Viking field systems, in Cleveland, although it may yet be established that the Scamridge dykes (Page 35) were field boundaries from this period.

Brompton Church

The church of St. Thomas at Brompton near Northallerton contains one of the finest collections of Anglo-Danish hogbacks in the country. Five of these remain in the church and five can be seen in Durham Cathedral library.

Hogbacks are remarkable stone carvings which were used to mark graves in the 9th and 10thC and may have been pagan. The hogbacks, a fine Saxon crosshead and the shaft of a cross — on which birds are carved — were found in 1867 when improvements were being made to the chancel.

It seems possible that the church was originally founded in the 7thC in which case it would have been a simple structure of wood and thatch. Stone crosses in this and later centuries were used as focal points for itinerant priests, and Brompton seems to have been a cultural centre for the design of wheel-headed crosses.

The best evidence for settlements is place names. From these, it appears that the Angles held more land in the Tees Valley than on the moors: Ayton, Hutton, Stainton, Hilton and Stokesley derive their names from these settlers. Each group of Angles lived in their own village or "ham" and were protected by an enclosure or "tun".

When the Vikings started to settle, they gave rather different names to their villages. They used place names ending in "by" such as Danby — the village of the Danes, Ingleby — the village of the Angles, and Normanby — the village of the Norse.

Domestic Finds

Purely secular finds dating from this period are rare in Cleveland. Some pottery has been found at Hartlepool, Guisborough, Norton and Tollesby, and some Viking coins — including one minted in Samarkand — have been found in Goldsborough (Pages 51 & 129).

Anglo-Viking Sculpture

Notwithstanding the above, no less than 24 churches — in the County of Cleveland alone — contain sculptured stones from this period. These stones are usually fragments of Christian crosses, grave markers and grave covers. Good examples of crosses can be seen at Middleton, Hovingham (Page 63) and Lastingham (Page 62) but hogbacks — the name given to a type of 9th and 10thC grave marker — are best seen at Sockburn (Page 65), Brompton near Northallerton (Page 55) and Kirkdale (Page 13).

Church Architecture

Many churches in the area have stones set into the walls which go back to Anglo-Saxon times, but some have church towers and naves — the lower parts of which are wholly Anglo-Saxon. In these, the stonework, windows and doorways demonstrate the Pre-Conquest style of architecture and good examples can be seen at Billingham (Page 61), Norton and Hart.

Burial Grounds

These usually indicate the faith of those who lie buried in them. Grave goods have been found in the pagan cemeteries at Hob Hill near Saltburn (Page 60), Norton (Page 64) and Kildale (Page 57). The east-west orientation of graves in the burial grounds found at Hartlepool Headland (Page 59) indicate that these people had been converted to Christianity.

Kildale Church

Kildale and its church are mentioned in the Domesday Survey of 1086, but the village was an ancient settlement even before the arrival of the Conqueror.

The church of St. Cuthbert's — seen in the photograph — was rebuilt as recently as 1868. The previous church dated back to 1714 but J.W. Ord in his "History and Antiquities of Cleveland" of 1846 wrote that this church included fragments of graves taken from the previous church and these fragments may have come from the ancient chapel of St. Kilda.

During the most recent rebuilding of the church in 1868 eight graves of Viking settlers were found. The grave goods included swords, axes, spears and a knife and buckle. A small balance was also unearthed which indicated that the Vikings were traders as well as raiders. These finds used to be displayed in the church but have been lost.

The railway alongside the church is the Esk line to Whitby.

Hogback from Brompton Church

Hartlepool's Anglo-Saxon Monastery

The Venerable Bede wrote in 731 AD that Hieu — the first woman in Northumbria to become a nun — founded a monastery at Hartlepool called Hereuteu.

The exact site of this monastery is not known but in 1833 house building in South Crescent — on the right hand edge of the photograph — revealed a cemetery with grave markers inscribed with a cross and a name.

One of these markers is kept in the choir of St. Hilda's Church and dates from the 7thC. It seems possible that the burials found in the 1970's near Church Walk — just below the church — came from the same cemetery although no grave markers were found.

The current excavations at Church Close — just above the church — have revealed further evidence of the monastery, but the foundations of its church probably lie beneath the present church.

The monasteries at Hartlepool and Whitby were run on similar lines for both men and women. Some time in the 9thC both monasteries seem to have suffered the same fate — total destruction by the Vikings.

The Cemetery at Hob Hill Saltburn

Over fifty Anglo-Saxon burial urns were recovered from what is now a golf course as a result of surface ironstone mining by Pease & Partners in 1909.

The graves were found in three lines running across the photograph. They were dated between the latter half of the 4thC and the end of the 6thC and represent one of the earliest Anglo-Saxon finds in the north of England.

Apart from the urns, a primitive coffin and some skeletons were found. One body had been wrapped in a large piece of hide and it is known that Anglo-Saxon warriors were often buried in this way — having been carried home from battle tightly sewn into such a hide.

There were many finds alongside the human remains, notably beads of jet, necklaces of coloured glass, bronze brooches, three knives, a spearhead and a Frankish throwing axe. Some of these can be seen in the Dorman Museum in Middlesbrough.

All the urns were in fragments and one explanation for this is that they were broken at the time of internment so that the souls of the dead could more readily join Woden when he came to "Hobitt" hill to claim them in his longship.

Billingham Church

According to Simeon of Durham — who was a chronicler in the early 12thC — the tower of St. Cuthbert's in Billingham became a place of refuge whenever raiders from Denmark or Scotland descended upon the village.

The earth bank, which protected the church and the village in Anglo-Saxon times, may have played a part in the Battle of Billingham Bottoms in 798 AD.

It seems slightly incongruous that a town as modern as Billingham should have such a very ancient history but there is evidence that a church and village were on this site in the late 7thC. A name stone from this period can be seen in the church.

The original church played a part in the spread of Christianity throughout the north of England. Tradition has it that the monks from Lindisfarne brought the bones of St. Cuthbert to Billingham at the time of the Viking raids between 875 and 883 AD.

Some of the old stone carvings found in the church proved so important that they have been displayed elsewhere. A fragment of an 8thC tombstone is in the British Museum and part of an 11thC cross is in the Monk's Dormitory at Durham Cathedral.

In Norman times the importance of St. Cuthbert's was rivalled by the Benedictine Monastery of Beaulieu (Bewley) on the outskirts of the village but — apart from a few stones — no trace of this monastery remains.

The Shrine of St. Cedd

The early history of the church at Lastingham — near Hutton-le-Hole — comes to us from the Venerable Bede who completed his "History of the English Church and People" in 731 AD, when he was a monk in the monastery at Jarrow. He tells us that St. Cedd founded a monastery at Lastingham in a place "more suitable for the dens of robbers and haunts of wild beasts than for human habitation".

The Vikings destroyed this monastery in the 9th or 10thC, but a later church was built on the site in which St. Cedd's body was re-interred.

In 1078 Stephen — The Abbot of Whitby — built the new apsed church of St. Mary's seen in the photograph. He started by building the crypt as a shrine to St. Cedd and this shrine is unique — being the only apsed crypt with side aisles in England. It is one of those special places in the area with an atmosphere of Christianity which echoes down nine centuries.

The 9thC crosshead, which can be seen in the crypt, was part of what must have been one of the largest Pre-Conquest monuments in the country. The diameter could have been over 5ft. (2m) supported on a shaft 24ft. (8m) high.

Hovingham Hall & Church

The Worsley family's association with All Saints Church at Hovingham goes back to the 16thC and unlike many similar associations, is still a strong one

All Saints is everything a parish church should be. It was probably re-built — after a Viking raid — by a landowner called Orm who also rebuilt St. Gregory's Minister at Kirkdale (Page 13). His masons incorporated old crosses into the tower and the one above the west door is 8thC Anglian. It has four equal arms and flaring ends and is among the oldest surviving Christian relics in the area.

The free standing Anglo-Saxon cross, mounted in a wrought iron frame behind the altar, is one of the best presented 10thC crosses in the country. Originally it would have stood on a round column in the open air and acted as a focal point for visiting preachers.

All Saints also has a unique Anglo-Saxon stone carving of eight figures standing in round-headed panels. The stone may have been a massive lintel over the doorway of an earlier church but now acts as a reredos.

Hovingham Hall — seen in front of the church — was built in the 1750's and 60's. The 4th Baronet — Sir William Worsley was one of the last Lord Lieutenants of the North Riding, and his daughter Katherine is the Duchess of Kent.

The Cemetery at Norton

The Anglo-Saxon cemetery in this photograph was excavated in 1984 and 1985 and found to be the largest pagan burial ground in the north of England.

It was discovered when children, who were swinging on trees alongside Mill Lane, uncovered a skull. The lane can be seen on the left of the dual carriageway which leads into the centre of Norton at the top of the photograph. The archaeological huts and the spoil tip can be seen at the edge of the excavation.

Glass beads, spears and shields were found during the work in 1984 and these indicated that the settlement had been relatively wealthy. Tests on the skeletons showed that the villagers were healthy and had died from natural causes. The cemetery dates to the early Anglo-Saxon period between 450 and 650 AD.

At the time of writing 120 skeletons have been found and it is hoped that an Anglo-Saxon settlement might be found nearby.

An exhibition of the finds from this cemetery can be seen in the library at Norton.

Sockburn Ruins

In the most southerly loop of the Tees — shaped like a sock — is Sockburn Hall which is a Victorian house built on the site of an old manor house.

Below the hall and partly obscured by trees — lie the ruins of the ancient church of All Saints. The church is mentioned in connection with the consecration of Archbishop Eanbald in 797 AD and the nave may date from that time. If so, this would make it one of the oldest naves in the area. The windows, arches and arcades belong to a later period but the massive long and short work — at the south-east and north-west corners of the building — appear to be original.

Sockburn has a very comprehensive collection of Anglo-Viking carvings. The shafts of the crosses are carved with figures of warriors, hunters and women and some of these have been identified as Valkyries welcoming the fallen warriors to Valhalla.

There are also a number of richly decorated hogbacks — some of an early date with naturalistic details — and one of a later date with a more stylistic treatment. One huge hogback is carved with a scene which seems to have been derived from the Scandinavian legend in which Tyr sacrificed his hand to Venrir — the great Wolf.

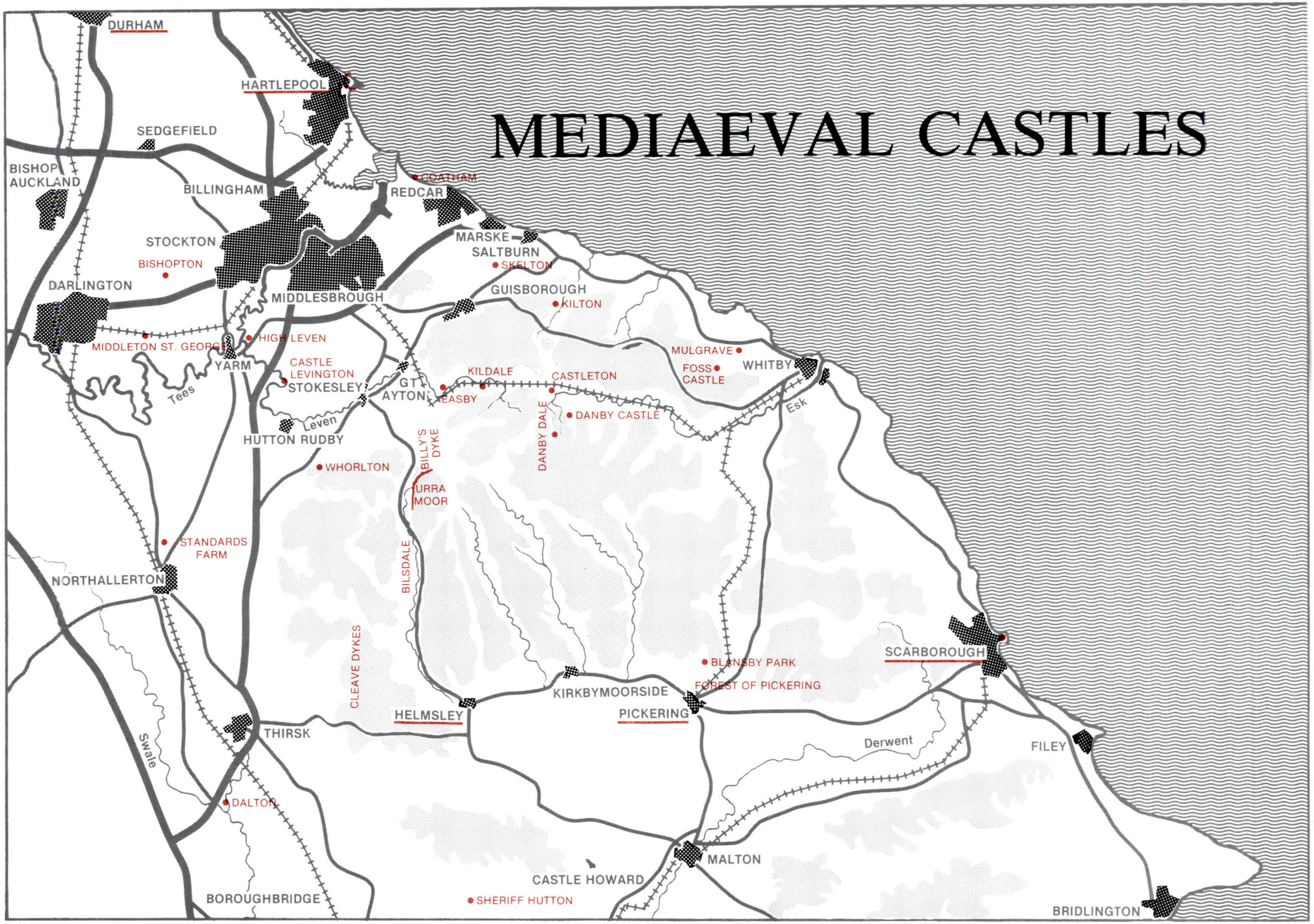
MEDIAEVAL CASTLES
DURHAM
HARTLEPOOL
SEDGEFIELD
BISHOP AUCKLAND
BILLINGHAM
COATHAM
REDCAR
STOCKTON
BISHOPTON
MARSKE
SALTBURN
SKELTON
DARLINGTON
MIDDLESBROUGH
GUISBOROUGH
KILTON
MIDDLETON ST. GEORGE
HIGH LEVEN
YARM
CASTLE LEVINGTON
STOKESLEY
GT AYTON
EASBY
KILDALE
CASTLETON
MULGRAVE
FOSS CASTLE
WHITBY
Tees
Leven
Esk
HUTTON RUDBY
DANBY CASTLE
DANBY DALE
BILLY'S DYKE
WHORLTON
URRA MOOR
STANDARDS FARM
NORTHALLERTON
BILSDALE
CLEAVE DYKES
SCARBOROUGH
BLANSBY PARK
FOREST OF PICKERING
KIRKBYMOORSIDE
HELMSLEY
PICKERING
THIRSK
Swale
Derwent
FILEY
DALTON
MALTON
CASTLE HOWARD
SHERIFF HUTTON
BOROUGHBRIDGE
BRIDLINGTON

CHAPTER VI

Prehistoric	Bronze Age	Iron Age	Romans	Danes	Middle Ages	Modern

CONQUEST & CONSOLIDATION

1066 to 1539

The Great Keep, Scarborough

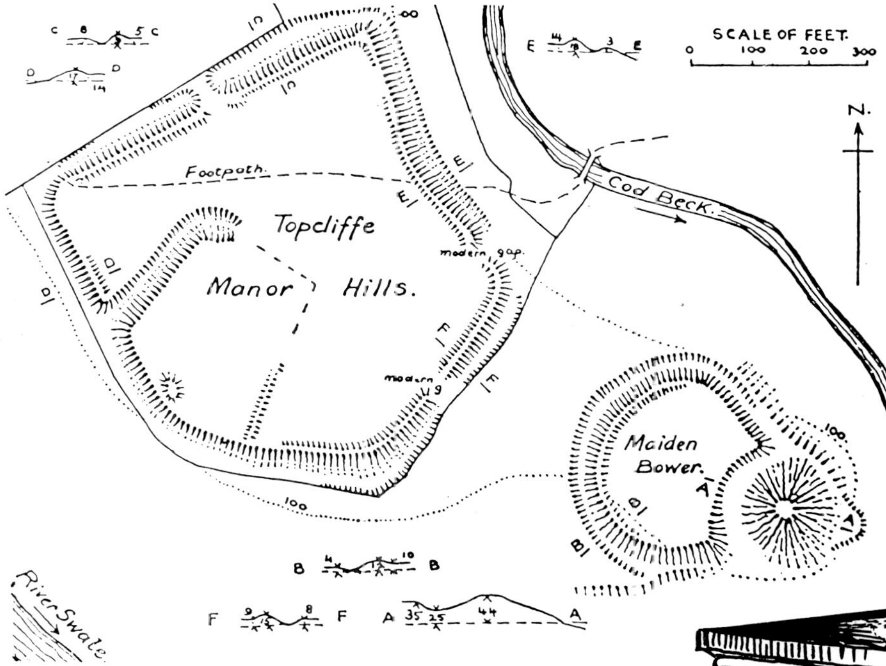

Dalton Motte and Bailey in 19thC

The Brus Monument, Guisborough

When the Conqueror took England in his iron grasp all the advantages of strong central government — last experienced under the Romans — were felt again. But whereas the Romans had reduced many of the British to slaves the Normans reduced many of the British — or more accurately the English — to serfs.

In this period violent events occured all round the world. The crusaders attempted to wrest the Holy Land from the Moslems and in the process killed more Christians and Jews than Arabs, the Mongol hordes under Genghis Khan killed two thirds of the people of Persia and established a vast empire stretching from Turkey to China which left nothing behind it when its conqueror died. The Black Death killed half of the people of Europe and Ivan the Great subjugated all of Russia under Moscow. In Japan the Samurai warriors defeated their rivals and in Peru the Incas won an empire.

In England the period can conveniently be said to begin with the conquest in 1066 and to end with the Dissolution of the Monasteries in 1539. The Feudal System — which was officially abolished in England only in 1661 — was based on the simplistic doctrine that all land belonged to the King who granted it to others in return for services. Such a doctrine could only be imposed and maintained by force and this entailed the construction of castles. In the course of time the power of the provincial Barons rivalled that of the King and it was not until the Wars of the Roses that the Tudor monarchs re-asserted their authority. The strong central government which the Tudors established was to prove of great benefit to England in a period when nationalism was beginning to dominate the politics of Europe.

The north of England was the last region to yield to the Conqueror and the first to rise against him. This rising was in 1069 when the forces of King Swein of Denmark joined the forces of Edgar the Atheling. The Conqueror brought his army up to York where he proceeded to harry the north. There has never been anything like the harrying: its effects were more fatal and far reaching than a nuclear explosion of the 20thC. Approximately 100,000 people perished and the devastation of the countryside north of York as far as the Tyne was almost total.

Seventeen years later when the Domesday Survey of 1086 took place most of the Anglo Danish villages in the Langbaurgh Wapentake were described as waste. Ingleby Greenhow near Great Ayton, was one of the few exceptions: in the time of Edward the Confessor it had been valued at £48 but it was assessed as being worth no more than 40 shillings in the Domesday Book. Of all his crimes against humanity the Conqueror is said to have repented of the harrying on his death bed. That was no consolation to the British, Celts, Romans, Angles and Danish inhabitants whose genetic lines were permanently severed by the extinguishing of all races in that area.

"Billy's Dyke"

A 2½ mile long dyke runs along the far edge of Urra Moor seen in the foreground. For most of its length it follows the 1200ft. (400m) contour which is where the edge of Bilsdale meets the moor.

The northern extremity of the dyke can be seen bottom right. It consists of a ditch on the dale side of the rampart and a dry stone wall on the moor side.

The purpose of this dyke is not known. It differs from the Cleave Dykes — between Sutton Bank and Osmotherley — which appear to be field boundaries but it also differs from the Scamridge Dykes — between Pickering and Scarborough — which might be "parish" boundaries (Page 35). It could have been a mediaeval deer park dyke.

Tradition has it that the Bilsdale Dyke was constructed by farmers living in the dale in order to prevent William the Conqueror from entering the dale from Urra Moor. It is thought that he used this route when returning to York from an expedition against the English stronghold in the Coatham marshes, so the tradition may have some substance to it.

Early Castles

The Conqueror devastated the north by the use of ring fortifications and motte and bailey castles. In the first instance these were earthen mounds with wooden towers and were the equivalent of the Roman marching camps. Examples of these defensive structures in their original form can be seen at Dalton (Page 79), Castle Levington (Page 78), Easby, Castleton, Middleton St. George, High Leven, Bishopton (Page 71) and Foss Castle. There is a strange mound in Danby Dale which may be another.

Stone Castles

Some time after the harrying, many of the early castles were strengthened in order to maintain a permanent hold on the surrounding countryside. The usual procedure was to replace the wooden towers and palisades with stone towers and stone 'curtain' walls and the area has many good examples of these 12thC and 13thC castles. The castles at Scarborough (Page 75), Danby, Mulgrave (Page 76), Pickering (Page 73), the original castle at Skelton (Page 83) and Kilton all belong to this category but research on this last castle has made it clear that subordination of the local peasantry was not their only purpose. They were also used to defend the area against invasions by the Danes and Scots, as were the walls at Hartlepool (Page 80).

Standards Farm, near Northallerton, was the site of the Battle of the Standard in 1138. Had the English branch of the Brus family lost this battle against the Scots the border between the two countries might well have become the Tees.

Later Castles

The final stage of castle building in this period took place in the 14thC and 15thC and is characterised by the keeps at Whorlton (Page 81), Sheriff Hutton (Page 82) and the striking remains of Helmsley Castle (Page 77). In this last case improvements in design, such as drum towers, were inspired by a crusader returning from the Continent.

Such castles acted as a refuge for local people during the Wars of the Roses and the Civil Wars of the 17thC when many of them were demolished by the cannon fire of Cromwell's soldiers. The castles which fell to Cromwell were deliberately slighted in order to break the power of provincial rivals to central government.

Motte & Bailey at Bishopton

The village of Bishopton lies between Stockton and Darlington and is the site of one of the best motte and bailey castles in the area.

It is considerably smaller than Dalton (Page 79) but is in an excellent state of preservation considering it is 800 years old.

The Conyers family held Bishopton from 1140 for at least five centuries. This family probably constructed the castle, which is a 12thC structure, rather than one thrown up during the Norman Conquest in the 11thC.

The motte itself is made of local clay and stone and is 45ft. (15m) high although Hutchinson — an 18thC authority — somehow managed to measure it as 60ft. (20m). Both motte and bailey were protected by moats which were fed from Bishopton Beck — running along the top of the photograph. There appears to be a ditch — dividing the bailey into half — which is an unusual feature for a fortification of this type.

Surtees — a 19thC authority — refers to a local tradition that the castle was built on a much older structure such as "a Danish fort, a Roman agger or a Druid temple" — but nothing has been found to substantiate this.

Turret at Kilton Castle

Pickering Castle

Originally this castle was a typical motte and bailey castle erected by the Conqueror in order to subjugate the area but it must also have helped to repel Viking raiders. It was erected at the natural crossing point of the east-west route along the northern edge of the Vale of Pickering, and the north-south route across the marshes to Malton.

The castle was extended and had its palisade replaced by a stone curtain wall in 1326 by Edward II in order to keep out the Scots, who were led by Robert de Brus. However its most usual function during the 12thC and 13thC was to act as a centre for deer and wild boar hunting in the forest of Pickering and in Blansby Park.

On hunting visits the Kings of England were accommodated in the New Hall — seen below the motte — and they worshipped in the chapel to the right of the motte.

Those who were found guilty of poaching or "assarting" were imprisoned in the King's Prison alongside the chapel.

One end of the picturesque North Yorkshire Moors Railway can be seen at the bottom of the photograph.

Castle Cliff Scarborough

After the Battle of the Standard in 1138 William le Gros — the Earl of Yorkshire — chose this superb natural site as the place to build his castle.

The main building of this castle was a gate tower which stood at the end of a curtain wall, close to the present keep. When Henry II came to the throne he seized Scarborough Castle as part of his policy of reducing the power of the barons. He appointed the Archbishop of York as his governor and built the keep in place of the gate tower. He also constructed an inner bailey by cutting off the western corner of the headland, by means of the bank and ditch seen in the photograph.

The exceptionally long curtain wall which runs the full length of the headland — and is seen more clearly on the front cover — was a great expense borne by Henry II and King John.

Throughout the later Middle Ages the castle was repeatedly attacked by the Scots and French. It changed hands twice in the Civil Wars — without a shot being fired — but finally fell to Parliament after the barbican and keep had been opened up by cannon fire.

Old Mulgrave Castle

The old castle of Mulgrave was built in about 1200 by Robert de Turnham and was the successor to Foss Castle nearby, which was a motte and bailey castle built in the 11thC.

It was constructed on a narrow wooded ridge between two parallel valleys — with two deep ditches across the ridge — and consists of a central keep and polygonal curtain wall. Its most obvious feature is a large 16thC window.

During the Civil Wars its defenders realised that it would not withstand Cromwell's cannons so they surrendered it in 1645 and it was slighted two years later.

The modern Mulgrave Castle (Page 139) lies a mile to the east — in the direction of the shadow of the microlight.

Helmsley Castle

Although the original castle was probably constructed in the middle of the 12thC no traces of it have been found. The present castle was exceptionally well designed by Robert de Roos, who was Lord of Helmsley from 1186 to 1227.

Robert de Roos was an experienced soldier who had learnt his craft in the struggle to retain Normandy for King John. His innovations included the drum towers on the six corners and on the sides of the main gate, which enabled the defenders to fire on attackers attempting to scale the walls.

The only recorded siege was in 1644 during the Civil Wars, when Sir John Crosland defended the castle for the King against Sir Thomas Fairfax. He held out for three months, but after his surrender the castle was slighted.

Castle Levington

The castle was an earthen mound with a timber palisade built high above the River Leven — which can be seen running along the left hand side of the photograph. The mound has a dished appearance which was originally formed by a ring of earth. The castle was protected on its western side by a ditch.

Levington was called Lenton in the Domesday Book of 1086 but there was no mention of a castle at that time.

The manor of Lenton was granted to Robert de Brus in the early 12thC and it seems likely that it was he who had the castle built. An account of 1274 refers to the "herbage in the round dyke" being worth half a mark yearly.

No trace of the village of Castle Levington remains, but in the 1940's an RAF aerial survey showed some mediaeval earthworks around White House Farm nearby.

Motte & Bailey at Dalton

This superb motte and its double bailey three miles south of Thirsk is one of the best examples of its kind in the north of England. It stands at the edge of the World War II airfield of Dalton and is a well know sight to the fliers in the Vale of York.

The Maiden's Bower — as it is called — lies between the River Swale in the background and its tributary Cod Beck on the left. It is believed to have been built by William de Percy in 1071. This sort of castle could be constructed in as little as three days by people working 18 hours a day "to save their lives". This compares quite favourably with what can be achieved today with modern earth moving machinery!

We know that the castle was fortified — probably with wooden palisades rather than stone walls — by Geoffrey Bishop Elect of Lincoln in 1174. At that time it was known as the castle of Toppecliva (Topcliffe).

There appears to be another motte and bailey — of a strange rectangular kind — on the right hand side of the outer bailey. The terracing on the side of the main motte was cut in modern times.

Hartlepool's Mediaeval Wall

The Headland of Hartlepool is a natural defensive area similar to, although not as good as, the headland of Scarborough (front cover).

In 1306 Robert de Brus claimed the Scottish throne and Hartlepool became one of the main supply points for the English armies and naval vessels. In 1316 the Scots pushed as far south as the Tees and burned the town, while its inhabitants watched in safety from ships offshore.

This was not to be endured and soon afterwards a limestone wall was built on the seaward side of the headland, and a chain was installed across the bar to prevent the entrance of hostile vessels. Excavations in 1983 established that this wall continued across the peninsula and archaeologists discovered a substantial bank and ditch, which had served as an earlier defence.

In 1346 five vessels were provided by Hartlepool for the seige of Calais which indicates the importance of the town at the time.

The remains of the town walls and the watergate can be seen at the bottom of the photograph to the left of the jetty. In 1836 the north gate was demolished and since then the mediaeval walls have survived only where they could serve as sea walls.

Whorlton Castle

After the Conquest Whorlton was one of the few villages which were not entirely wasted in the harrying. A good deal of 14thC material about the village is available and it covers the period when the gatehouse — seen in the photograph — was constructed. The most recent castle was built by Robert de Meynell and its surviving gatehouse has carved shields of the Meynell, D'Arcy and Gray families over its archway.

The Earl of Lennox lived here in the 16thC. His son Darnley married Mary Queen of Scots and there is reason to believe that some of the plots, which brought about that unfortunate marriage, were hatched at Whorlton Castle.

The motte is rather square in shape and covers an area of three quarters of an acre. It may have been widened to accommodate a stone keep which has since been pulled down. The rectangular bailey can just be seen beyond the road.

Sheriff Hutton Castle

The keep of this castle is one of the most impressive in the north of England. Only its four corners remain but their gaunt shapes dominate the village and the countryside around.

The original castle on the high mound was built by Bertram de Bulner, who was Sheriff of Yorkshire, and gave the village its name. The last castle was built in the 14thC by John Neville whose family arms can be seen above the 15thC gateway.

The castle is known as the place in which the first book to be printed in England by Caxton was translated into English. The translator was Anthony Woodville — the brother of Edward IV. He was a guardian of little Prince Edward who was murdered in the tower of London.

Warwick the Kingmaker lived here and Elizabeth of York was imprisoned here by her uncle who became Richard III. She survived to become the wife of Henry VII, the first Tudor King and the man, who more than any other, took England out of the Middle Ages.

In 1941 Arthur Mee wrote about this castle in his "Kings of England". He deplored the fact that the courtyard of a castle — which had seen such great days — should be used as a common farmyard. It still serves that purpose.

Skelton Castle

The original manor and castle of Skelton were granted to Robert de Brus in about 1100. Although Robert de Brus did not take part in the Battle of Hastings, he supported the Conqueror's youngest son Henry against his cousin Odo, and was rewarded with 94 lordships in Yorkshire — 51 of them in the North Riding. This made him one of the greatest lords in the north of England.

At the Court of the Conqueror, David — the future King of Scotland — became a close friend of Robert de Brus and granted him many more lordships across the border. The Scottish possessions were later to divide the loyalties of the Brus family.

Robert de Brus made Skelton Castle his headquarters. Either he or his predecessor enclosed it with a vast moat no less than 240ft. (80m) wide. The castle remained in his family for many generations but eventually came into the hands of the Wharton family who still own it.

In the 1790's John Wharton — following the fashion of the day — rebuilt the castle in Gothic style. No trace of the earlier castle survives.

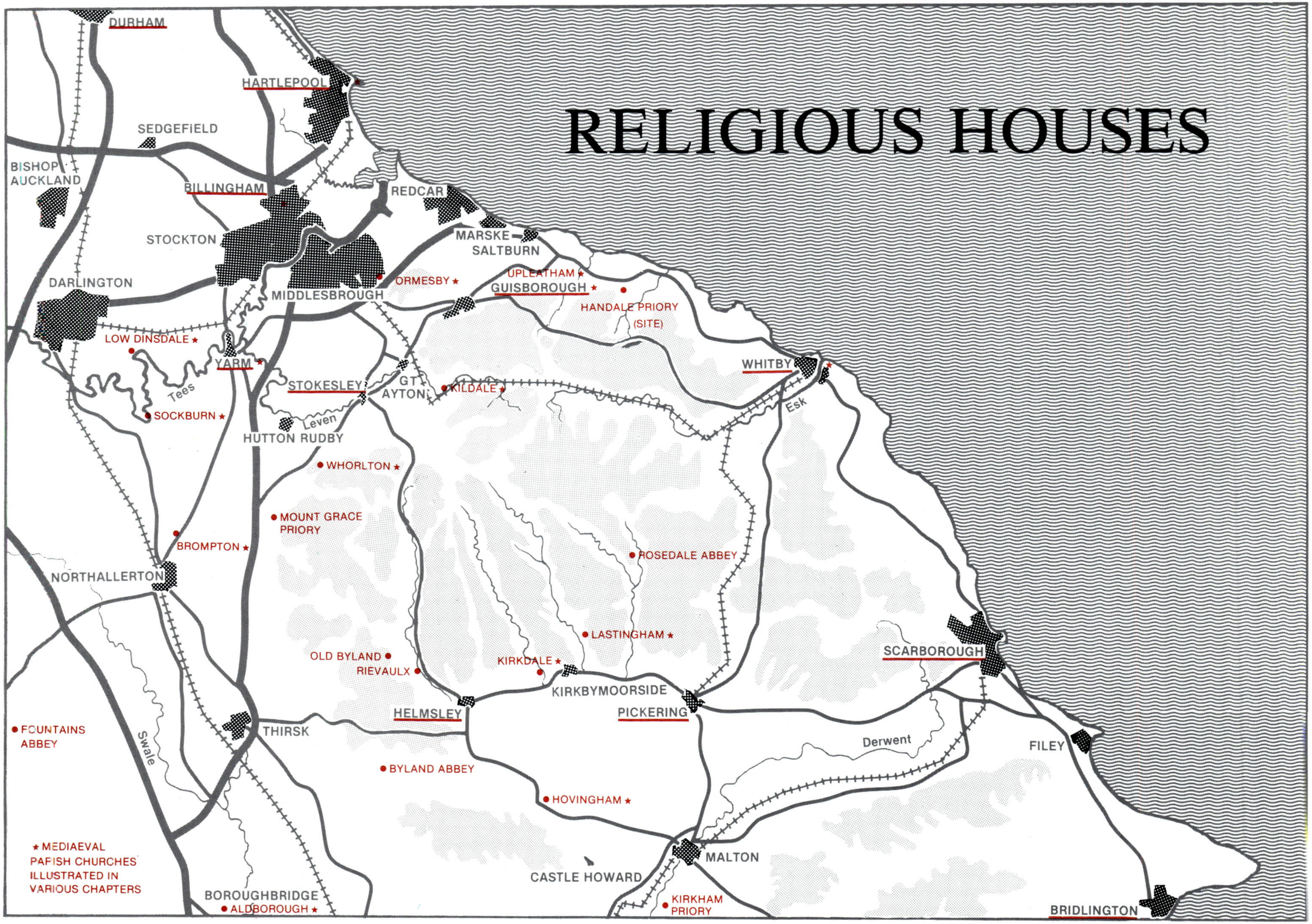
RELIGIOUS HOUSES
DURHAM
HARTLEPOOL
SEDGEFIELD
BISHOP AUCKLAND
BILLINGHAM
REDCAR
STOCKTON
MARSKE
SALTBURN
DARLINGTON
UPLEATHAM ★
ORMESBY ★
GUISBOROUGH ★
MIDDLESBROUGH
HANDALE PRIORY (SITE)
LOW DINSDALE ★
YARM ★
WHITBY
STOKESLEY
GT AYTON
KILDALE ★
Tees
SOCKBURN ★
Leven
Esk
HUTTON RUDBY
WHORLTON ★
MOUNT GRACE PRIORY
BROMPTON ★
ROSEDALE ABBEY
NORTHALLERTON
LASTINGHAM ★
SCARBOROUGH
OLD BYLAND
RIEVAULX
KIRKDALE ★
KIRKBYMOORSIDE
PICKERING
HELMSLEY
FOUNTAINS ABBEY
THIRSK
Swale
Derwent
FILEY
BYLAND ABBEY
HOVINGHAM ★
★ MEDIAEVAL PARISH CHURCHES ILLUSTRATED IN VARIOUS CHAPTERS
MALTON
CASTLE HOWARD
BOROUGHBRIDGE
ALDBOROUGH ★
KIRKHAM PRIORY
BRIDLINGTON

CHAPTER VII

Prehistoric	Bronze Age	Iron Age	Romans	Danes	Middle Ages	Modern

MASTERPIECES IN STONE

1066 to 1539

Byland Abbey

Durham Cathedral

The first, and arguably the first of only two great periods of English architecture, came about as a result of the strong central government imposed by the Conqueror.

The violent events around the world described in the last chapter were followed by an explosion of reconstruction during which some of the greatest stone buildings in the world were conceived and executed. In the Moslem world the domes and minarets of the most magnificent mosques were perfected and in the Christian world the Romanesque style — which had been based on classical principles — developed into the graceful arches of the Gothic style. In Africa the mysterious stone city of Zimbabwe was built and in Peru the finest Inca temples — now overgrown by jungle — were constructed. From China Marco Polo brought news of the pleasure domes decreed by Kubla Khan and it was not long after that that the Emperors of the Sung Dynasty rebuilt the Great Wall.

In England great churches and monasteries were erected to the glory of God. To this day cathedrals such as Salisbury, Lincoln, Ely, Winchester, Canterbury, York and Durham dominate the towns lying at their feet both literally and also in terms of concept, materials and skill.

Some Anglo-Saxon churches were added to, but most were rebuilt entirely in stone. Prosperity and an increasing population led to the addition of aisles and bell towers. The simple pointed arch of the Early English style gave way — at the beginning of the 14thC — to the Decorated style with its double pointed arches. By the end of that century the Perpendicular style had developed and the hallmarks of this were graceful fan vaulted roofs and long stone mullions running the full height of the windows and columns.

These stylistic developments in church architecture also applied to the monasteries. From the late 11thC — when the monastic revival took place — the three most important orders were the Benedictine, Augustinian and Cistercian. The monasteries of these orders gradually adopted a standard building plan consisting of a central cloister with church, chapter house (business office) and frater (dining hall) on three sides of the cloister. Members of the smaller Carthusian order on the other hand lived in separate cells and had a small church. The best of these monasteries would no doubt be standing today if the Tudor monarchs had not been so determined to be masters in their own house. As it was Henry VIII objected to the abbots and priors — who controlled some of the best estates in his realm — because they looked to leadership from Rome rather than London. Nationalism, and not spiritualism, was the rising force of the day and the English monasteries were pulled down.

Monasteries

The north of England was not only a battle field on which Kings, Barons, Danes and Scots resolved their differences, it was also the home of the Lindisfarne branch of Christianity and the area in which some of the country's greatest churches and monasteries were built.

Rievaulx Abbey

These spectacular ruins in their superb setting got their name from "valley of the River Rye". They are all that remain of the first Cistercian abbey in the north, but in 1131 — just before the abbey's foundation — a monk described the site as a "place of horror and waste solitude".

The church and principal buildings around the cloister were finished by 1175. From about this date the three Cistercian abbeys of Rievaulx, Byland and Fountains underwent many developments until their Dissolution in 1538.

At the far side of the site is the abbey's church which was known for its severe nave and beautiful choir stalls in the Early English style. The building to the left was the frater — or dining hall — which in the early 14thC must have been a magnificent hall. It was 115ft. (40m) long with a seven-sided rafter roof, delicate coloured marble columns, a floor of chequered tiles, and walls finished in hard lime with the false joints picked out in red.

The cloister lay between the frater and the church. Behind the high wall in the foreground was the monks reredorter with its row of wooden seats over a drain. The mediaeval monastery was truly a retreat from the harsh world outside!

In the north of the area covered by this book Durham Cathedral (Page 93) can claim to be one of the finest Romanesque churches in the world — it certainly has the best site. It was from this site that St. Cuthbert's followers spread the Christian gospel and by the 14thC the magnificent abbeys of Rievaulx (Page 87), Whitby (Page 94) and Byland (Page 91) had been founded. The priories of Guisborough (Page 92) and Mount Grace (Page 89) were not far behind. However other religious houses such as the abbey at Rosedale, the friary at Hartlepool (Page 95) and the priory at Handale can no longer be seen due to the thoroughness of their demolition and the zeal of stone thieves.

Churches

The most important mediaeval towns in the north of the area were Hartlepool, Yarm, Guisborough and Whitby, and in the south Helmsley, Pickering and Scarborough. The only mediaeval superstructures in these towns, which are still in use, are the churches although none of these are wholly mediaeval.

The churches of ancient Cleveland — from the air — would be a large enough subject for a book of its own, but as it happens many of these churches were photographed because they occupied the site of a stone age cave, mesolithic carr, an Anglo-Saxon or mediaeval building. They are indicated on the map at the beginning of this chapter and include the following;

Mount Grace Priory

Founded in 1397 this tranquil and romantic Carthusian monastery differed from other monasteries in England in that the monks resembled hermits living in seclusion, not only from the world, but also from each other.

As a result the buildings differed from other orders in that a separate cell was provided for each monk and a communal dormitory and dining hall were therefore not needed. However the space required for the fifteen individual cells and their gardens made the cloister much larger than usual. Mount Grace represents the best surviving example of a Carthusian plan in the country.

The ruin in the centre of the priory is that of the original church which was a plain aisle-less rectangle, and the only place in which monks came into contact with each other.

The large gabled building in the foreground once housed the stables and accommodated visitors; it was converted into a private house in 1654.

Like Guisborough Priory, Mount Grace escaped the Act of Suppression but in 1540 Prior Wilson and the other members of the order surrendered the house quietly and were granted pensions.

Guisborough Priory

Byland Abbey

The original site of this abbey, near Old Byland Village, was so close to Rievaulx that the bells of the two monasteries caused confusion.

Sometime around 1117 this second site was chosen by Cistercian monks who "began manfully to root out the woods, and by long and wide ditches to draw off the abundance of water from the marshes." The Cistercians were determined agriculturists.

The church of this abbey must have been very impressive. The west window — the base of which can be seen in the photograph — was a great wheel nearly 24ft. (8m) across.

The Cistercians originally reacted against the splendour and worldliness of the Clunic and Benedictine Orders, and the buildings on this site were plain and simple. The monks' vestments were not embroidered, the crosses were made of wood and the chandeliers of iron.

However the undoubted wealth of the Cistercians and other orders offended Henry VIII, and in 1539 Byland Abbey went the way of the other monasteries.

Guisborough Priory

The photograph shows the remains of the priory of St. Mary of Guisborough which was founded in 1119 for the Augustinian order by Robert de Brus. The Brus family cenotaph can be seen in the parish church on the left of the priory.

The original priory was destroyed in 1289 by a fire which was caused by a plumber who left his iron pans — filled with burning coals — on the dry roof beams.

It was rebuilt and for a hundred years 'enjoyed' a reputation for great strictness, but by the end of that time the Archbishop discovered that there was "too much straying from the cloister and loose discourse in recreation times", and some of the monks were sent to the Bridlington and Kirkham abbeys for correction.

In 1535 Guisborough Priory was the fourth richest in Yorkshire after York, Fountains and Selby and therefore escaped the Act for the Suppression of the Lesser Monasteries. As a result Prior Pursglove continued to keep his "pompous house" — with 400 dependent households — until the Dissolution four years later.

The priory represents a landmark in the development of Gothic architecture in the north. The east window was recognised, in its time, as one of the finest in the country.

Durham Cathedral

On the northern edge of the area covered by this book stands what is arguably the most magnificent Romanesque cathedral in Europe.

It was to this site — Dunholm in a loop of the Wear — that monks carried the exhumed remains of St. Cuthbert who had originally been buried at Lindisfarne on the Northumbrian coast. This brotherhood of monks was responsible for the spread of Christianity throughout the north of England including areas which are now Durham, Cleveland and North Yorkshire.

The cathedral was started in 1093 and famous though it became, the city was just as well known as a centre of learning. Its School of Divinity dates back to the 15thC.

The Norman castle, which can be seen beyond the cathedral, dates from 1070. It stands near the centre of the wall which once defended the neck of the peninsula against invasion by the Scots.

Whitby Abbey

The abbey church seen behind the modern coastguard station occupies a site as dramatic as Durham Cathedral's. It is not surprising that many Anglo-Saxon Kings and Queens chose this magnificent setting for their last resting place.

The original abbey was one of six which King Oswy of Northumbria swore to build in celebration of his great victory over the pagan King of Mercia in 655 AD. St. Hilda — the first abbess of Hartlepool — founded this abbey on a site which may be near that of the lost Roman signal station. Roman coins and 5thC pottery have been found here and Bede tells us that the original name of the abbey — Streonshalh — meant "haven of the watch tower".

It was here in 664 AD that the Synod of Whitby met and decided that English Christianity should follow the Roman path rather than the Irish. The Vikings sacked the monastery in 870 AD and the present mediaeval abbey was built in the 13thC.

Henry VIII "dissolved" it in 1539 but its church was still intact in 1711. Since then it has withstood great storms and a naval bombardment in 1914, but not the stone thieves.

The 12thC church to the right of the ruins is St. Mary's which has splendid Georgian pews and fittings. The stone building to the left is a strange and inaccessible edifice originally erected by the Cholmleys as a banqueting hall in the 17thC.

The Friary at Hartlepool

Many centuries after the monastery of Hartlepool had been destroyed by the Vikings, the brothers of the Franciscan order built a friary in the same area.

The massive church and the friary buildings lay on the site now occupied by "Friarage Field" which originally included the playing fields near Henry Smith School. Hartlepool Headland in the 13thC and 14thC was dominated by this church and the parish church of St. Hilda.

When the cemetery — lying to the north of the friary church — was excavated in 1983 150 burials were discovered. Pathological evidence showed that those buried had ranged in age from their early teens to their seventies. They had lived on a high protein diet, which was probably fish, and their teeth were good. Arthritis had deformed the limbs of some of them to an extent which is rarely reached in 20thC sufferers.

The Franciscans were an austere order noted for their care of the sick. They were expelled in 1539 when the 18 brothers and their keeper — Friar Richard Threlkeld — became victims of the "dissolution".

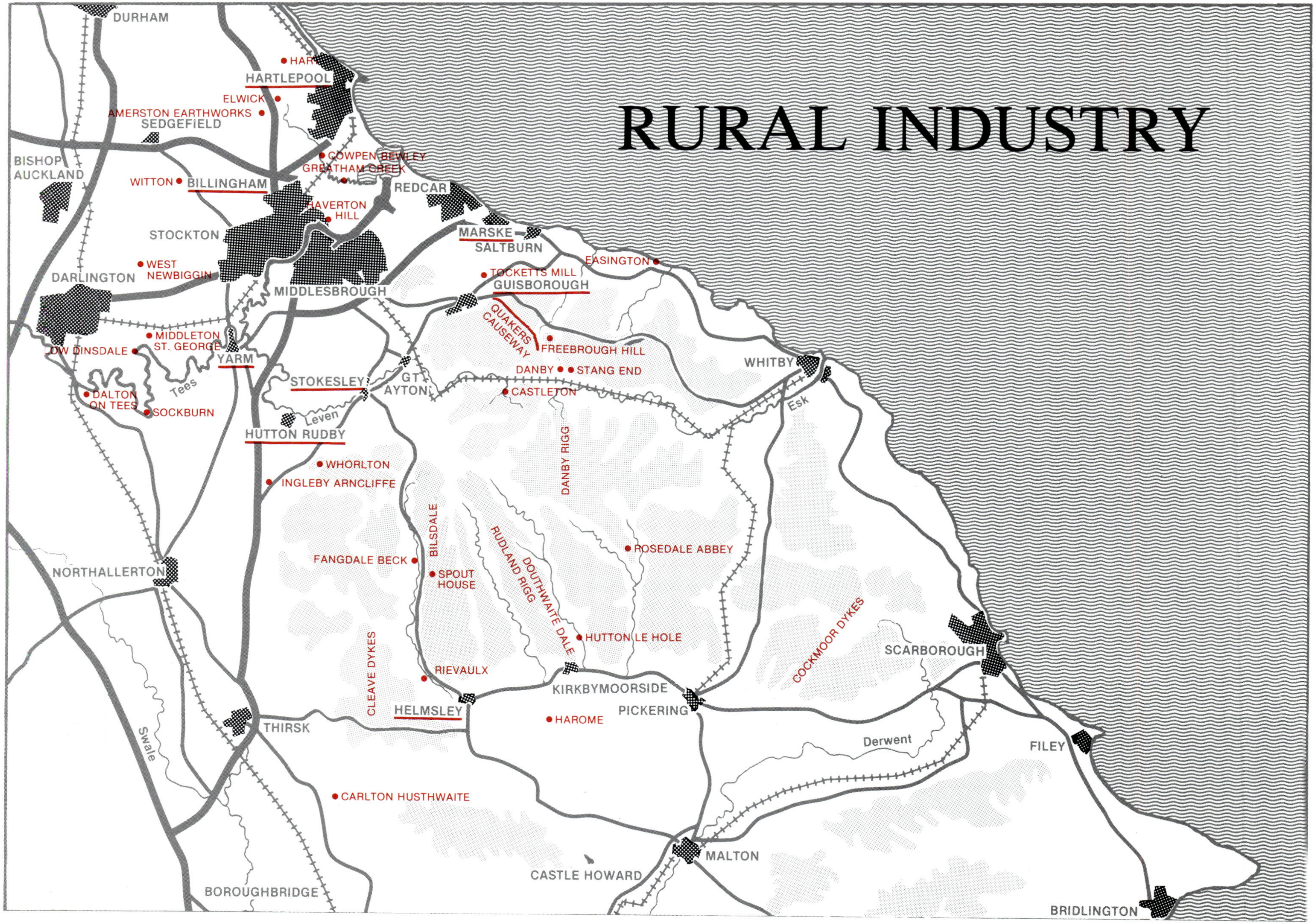
RURAL INDUSTRY
DURHAM
HAR
HARTLEPOOL
ELWICK
AMERSTON EARTHWORKS
SEDGEFIELD
BISHOP AUCKLAND
COWPEN BEWLEY
GREATHAM CREEK
WITTON
BILLINGHAM
REDCAR
HAVERTON HILL
STOCKTON
MARSKE
SALTBURN
WEST NEWBIGGIN
DARLINGTON
EASINGTON
TOCKETTS MILL
GUISBOROUGH
MIDDLESBROUGH
QUAKERS CAUSEWAY
MIDDLETON ST. GEORGE
OW DINSDALE
FREEBROUGH HILL
YARM
WHITBY
DANBY
STANG END
STOKESLEY
GT AYTON
CASTLETON
Tees
DALTON ON TEES
SOCKBURN
Leven
Esk
HUTTON RUDBY
WHORLTON
INGLEBY ARNCLIFFE
DANBY RIGG
BILSDALE
ROSEDALE ABBEY
FANGDALE BECK
SPOUT HOUSE
RUDLAND RIGG
DOUTHWAITE DALE
NORTHALLERTON
COCKMOOR DYKES
HUTTON LE HOLE
SCARBOROUGH
CLEAVE DYKES
RIEVAULX
KIRKBYMOORSIDE
HELMSLEY
PICKERING
HAROME
THIRSK
Swale
Derwent
FILEY
CARLTON HUSTHWAITE
MALTON
CASTLE HOWARD
BOROUGHBRIDGE
BRIDLINGTON

CHAPTER VIII

Prehistoric	Bronze Age	Iron Age	Romans	Danes	Middle Ages	Modern

MEDIAEVAL WAY OF LIFE

1066 to 1539

Hart Windmill 1930

The Bow Bridge, Castleton

The castles and cathedrals of the mediaeval period are so impressive that it is difficult to believe that most villagers lived close to the poverty line for much of their lives.

All over the world the business of living off the land — and being taxed to pay for protection of one kind or another — has been going on since the dawn of the Bronze Age. A level of taxation which removes too much of a farmer's surplus can reasonably be called exploitation but we know too little to be able to say whether life in the Sung Dynasty was more bearable than — say — life among the bog people in Denmark.

But we can be sure that war, fire, flood and plague brought immediate starvation and that there was no shortage of these all over the world. Plague was particularly prevalent in England during this period and the outbreak of bubonic plague in 1347 — known as the Black Death — destroyed half of the population. The resulting shortage of labour gave impetus to the adoption of new farming methods. The spread of learning from monasteries was to lead to the renaissance of classical knowledge, and the experiments of Francis Bacon in the 13thC are examples of this. Markets and the increase in farming surplus — although still meagre — encouraged the birth of a merchant class.

Eventually these trends were felt in the countryside. In the course of time the development of windmills and watermills to grind the corn benefitted the village and the building of bridges and inland ports aided the exchange of surplus. Fishponds, man-made rabbit warrens and deer parks improved the diet and released labour for new cultivation. The digging of moats around granaries and manors provided a cost effective way of protecting the surplus, and improved methods of mining and salt production allowed it to be exchanged for goods which improved the standard of living.

Mediaeval manor houses are familar to most of us but the longhouses of the ordinary people are not. The walls of longhouses were made of either cob, which was a mixture of clay, straw, sand and gravel or of wattle and daub, which was a mesh of thin branches covered with mud. The main frame and roof was of cruck construction which consisted of pairs of tree boughs set in — or on — the ground and jointed at the top. The roofs were thatched with straw or turf. Such houses were divided by a cross passage with the animals on one side and the farmer's family on the other.

Wind and Water Power

The limestone bedrock north of the Tees caused water to run away too fast for the use of watermills, so windmills were more common. Of the few which remain the best are at Hart and Elwick (Page 106) both near Hartlepool. There is an impressive series of watermills and mill races on Billingham Beck between Witton Mill and Billingham, but the best places to see working watermills are at Tocketts Mill near Guisborough and at Low Mill on Fangdale Beck in Bilsdale.

Crofts at Stokesley

All through the mediaeval period — for no less than four centuries — the Lords of the Manor of Stokesley were members of the Eures family. The Eures only left the village in 1622 but during most of this period the strip system prevailed in the outfields around the village. Only the Eures and the freemen were entitled to all that their strips produced.

The safety valve on this oppressive feudal system was the croft. Crofts — sometimes referred to as homesteads — lay behind each cottage. At the top of the photograph they are separated from the outfields by a back lane which still bears that name. The crofts may not have been owned by those living in the cottages, but the tenants were entitled to all they could produce.

Most mediaeval villages show the remains of crofts. They are the ribs of the villages upon which later generations built. As recently as 1894 the Ordnance Survey map of Stokesley showed almost nothing except streets, crofts and enclosed fields.

Causeways and Ports

Most country roads have developed from mediaeval tracks but the causeways — or pannier ways — on the moors show what these old tracks looked like. The moors abound with examples, but there is a particularly well preserved section (Page 105) running from Birkbrow near Guisborough in the direction of Danby.

Yarm on the Tees (Page 101) was a typical mediaeval river port, which enabled local farmers to exchange their surplus for goods from the Continent.

Fish, Conies and Venison

Most north-eastern villages had a fishpond for fish and waterfowl. Many can be seen in the villages between Helmsley and Scarborough and there are good examples at Dalton on Tees, Yarm and Elwick (Page 109). Dykes, to contain deer parks, were dug on the edge of the moors but can be mistaken for boundary and defensive dykes. There is no doubt that most of the dykes at Whorlton near Stokesley (Page 117) were deer park dykes. The pillow mounds to the south of the moors are probably the remains of artificial rabbit warrens and those near Hutton-le-Hole (Page 108) are particularly good examples. The earthworks at Amerston north of Billingham defy any of these explanations.

Moated Sites

Moats were dug in the 14thC both to protect farms and to lend prestige to their owners. Not many can be found in Durham and Cleveland, probably because they would have been ineffective against serious attacks by the Scots. However moats can still be seen at West Newbiggin near Sadberge, Low Dinsdale (Page 110) Hutton Rudby, Arncliffe Hall and Easington near Loftus.

Mining

Mining in the Middle Ages was on a small scale but bell pits provided an effective method of winning coal and iron ore. The bell pits on Rudland Rigg (Page 147) are good examples of the system although these probably belong to a later period. Salt was obtained by diverting sea water into 'salterns' — such as those at Greatham Creek near Cowpen Bewley (Page 107) — where the water was boiled away in large pans.

Yarm

This charming mediaeval market town — built in a loop of the Tees — has a history of great interest. "Yarum" was included in the Domesday Survey and in those days it only had a ford, which probably crossed the river above the site of the railway viaduct. This would have made Westgate more important than the High Street.

By the 14thC Yarm was an important port and the point from which goods, such as wool and lead, were exported. However recent excavations below the bridge have failed to locate the timbers of the old wharfs.

The bridge was built by the Bishop of Durham in 1405 and would have been demolished if a new cast iron bridge, completed in 1804, had not collapsed after a few months.

The promoters of the Stockton and Darlington Railway first met on 12th February 1820 at the "George & Dragon" in the High Street.

Thomas Meynell was Chairman of the promoters. His home at the time was the 18thC hall called the Friarage, which can be seen in the top right hand corner of the photograph. The Friarage was built on the site of a Dominican Friary founded in 1260, and is now Yarm School.

The railway viaduct was completed in 1851 and Henry Pease described it as "one of the finest works of the kind in the Kingdom".

Boundaries and Crofts

The dykes of the Cleave Dyke system are likely to be mediaeval boundaries between outfields or villages because legal records from this period make frequent reference to these dykes. The plots which men worked for themselves were known as crofts and these can be seen all over the area at any village with mediaeval origins — such as Stokesley (Page 99). They show up clearly in the aerial views of the deserted villages in Chapter IX and in the village plans in Chapter X.

Manors and Houses

The oldest mediaeval buildings of consequence in the area are Marske Hall and Ingleby Manor (Page 135) which were built during or just after the Tudor period. There is a stone cottage in Ingleby Arncliffe which may be a 14thC priest's house (Page 103) and a timber frame house at Carlton Husthwaite (Page 138) which is probably Elizabethan.

There was an old cottage at Stang End near Danby which has been rebuilt at the Ryedale Folk Museum at Hutton-le-Hole (Page 111) complete with its ingle nook and witch post. The longhouse next to the Sun Inn in Bilsdale, known as Spout House, (Page 104) has been restored to the condition which it was in as the Old Sun Inn. Its builders used the same construction method as was used for farmhouses in the Middle Ages.

The Priest's House Ingleby Arncliffe

This stone built cottage — known locally as the Monk's House — may be the oldest building in the area. There are references in a mediaeval document to a cottage in Ingleby Arncliffe, which was lived in by a priest in 1300, and this may be the cottage.

We know that the rectangular windows and the well ordered stonework at each end of the building dates from 1623 but the arched window on the first floor, and the stonework round it, appear to be earlier. In the 14thC the main door was beneath the arched window and the roof was thatched.

If this building was lived in by the village priest in the early 14thC he might have fallen a victim to the Black Death. About half of the Cleveland population died during this outbreak of bubonic plague in 1349 and parish priests, who conducted the funerals, were particularly susceptible to the disease.

Spout House

This 16thC house in Bilsdale is a typical cruckhouse of the type built by Yorkshire farmers for many hundreds of years. It lies on the Stokesley road to Helmsley not far from the Bilsdale television mast and has been restored to its original condition by the Committee of the North York Moors National Park.

All the fittings, such as the benches, tables and fireplace are original. On the first floor the old box beds are preserved under the thatched roof.

In the 18thC Spout House became the Sun Inn and was used by local farmers, jet miners and 'cloggers' who made their living by cutting clog soles from alder wood.

In 1823 the landlord of the Sun Inn was William Ainsley. Ever since then the landlords have all been William Ainsleys although the building in the foreground became the Inn in 1914.

Quakers Causeway Birkbrow

The ancient causeways of England are in a better state of preservation on the North York Moors and on the south Pennines than anywhere else in the country.

Paths — like the one down the centre of this photograph — were made from sandstone paving slabs and crossed the moors in the days before roadways. They made travel possible for man and pannier ponies and the goods they carried ranged from jet and alum to fish and illicit liquor.

Most of the causeways had mediaeval uses and this one was used by travellers between Guisborough Priory and the castle at Castleton. After crossing the Esk by the Bow Bridge they could travel on by another causeway to Rosedale Abbey.

The Quakers Causeway lies between the Bronze Age settlements near Freebrough Hill and those on Danby Rigg, and it seems likely that this route has prehistoric origins.

Elwick Windmill

In the whole of Cleveland County no windmill has been preserved in working order, and the few that remain are deteriorating fast.

Of the windmills which existed 50 years ago the two most complete examples are the tower mills at Hart and Elwick. Both were built over magnesian limestone which is too porous to hold enough water to drive watermills.

The slender brick tower of Elwick contains three sets of mill stones with driving gear, and these have been inaccessible since the lower floors of the building were removed.

The sails and the fantail can be seen to be missing. One of these sails was removed around the turn of the century in order to keep the older mill at Hart in working order.

The photograph shows that the windmill was constructed after the ridge and furrow had been formed — otherwise the building would have interfered with the straight furrow of the ox-team.

Saltworkings at Greatham Creek

The mounds seen in the loops of the creek are the remains of mediaeval salterns. The creek is Greatham Creek which meanders through the low lying ground between the Tees and Greatham.

This area was used for hundreds of years to produce salt for human consumption. It was obtained by burning sea coal — gathered from Hartlepool beach — under large pans of salt water. Most of the spoil around the saltern comes from the coke and ash left over after burning this sea coal.

In Victorian times the whole area from Greatham to Haverton Hill was covered with rigs which were used for drilling wells and pumping the brine from the salt bed 900ft. (300m) below the surface. Some of the output of Cerebos salt came from this area and production only ceased in 1970.

Nowadays thousands of tonnes of brine are pumped from the salt bed as part of the process for manufacturing chlorine and sodium products.

Pillow Mounds Hutton-le-Hole

At the end of the ridge of high ground between Hutton-le-Hole and Douthwaite Dale there are more than two dozen well defined mounds shaped like pillows. Each measures about 40ft. x 15ft. x 2ft. high. (13m x 5m x 70cm).

Pillow mounds of this kind are thought to have been rabbit warrens constructed by villagers in the Middle Ages when it was important to conserve any livestock which could provide fresh meat through the winter. However it seems strange that no documentary evidence has been discovered for these warrens.

Pillow mounds are usually found on poor light soil and rabbits do well on such soils. Half the Cockmoor Dykes — overlooking Trousdale near Pickering — are thought to have been constructed as warrens, and to have had nothing to do with similar dykes nearby.

Mediaeval villagers probably noticed that 'conies' burrowed into any new ditch and so they heaped up mounds of earth in a variety of different shapes.

Elwick Hall Fishpond

The fishpond in the foreground lies a few yards east of the A19 from Billingham to Newcastle and was originally built to meet the needs of Elwick Hall at the top of the photograph. The parish itself took the name Elwick Hall and it seems possible that this well constructed fishpond served the needs of a number of families.

Fishponds like this one were an important part of mediaeval life as there was little fresh meat to be had during the winter months, and fish were needed for Lent, Fridays and other days of abstinence.

This pond would have included fish breeding tanks, and the islands in the middle would have been used to protect ducks and geese from foxes.

Elwick Hall appears to be a fine 18thC house but it has a mediaeval central core which was added to by an incumbent of the parish church of St. Peter's.

The Moated Site at Low Dinsdale

In the 14thC it was quite common for men of prosperity to add great prestige — and a certain amount of protection — to their manors by means of a moat. Local maps show many moated sites but this one at Low Dinsdale is among the best.

The Domesday village of "Dirneshale" lies to the south of Middleton St. George in the same loop of the Tees as Sockburn (Page 65). It was held by Siward, Earl of Northumberland (mentioned by Shakespeare in 'Macbeth') who died in 1055. The estate then passed to the Surtees family, who were probably responsible for the moats and for the feeder ditch which can be seen running to the Tees in the middle distance. The moat is a double one on the far side of the house and the area has many interesting earthworks, the purpose of which will only be revealed by excavation.

Dinsdale Manor — within the moat — dates from the Tudor period and may have been built by Christopher Place who bought the estate from the Surtees in 1538. For some unrecorded reason he placed the Surtees Coat of Arms on his gateway and refused to move it, even when ordered to do so by the courts. These arms have been relocated on the bridge — seen on the nearside of the moat — and bear the words "Malo Mori Quam Foe Dari" (Death before Dishonour).

The church of St. John the Baptist — on the right of the photograph — was built in 1195 and contains some interesting Pre-Conquest carvings.

Ryedale Folk Museum Hutton le Hole

The Wheelhouse and Barn *(top building)*
This barn contains a threshing machine which was originally powered by horses driving an overhead wheel in a 5 sided wheelhouse adjoining the barn.

The Glass Furnace House
(building with 8-sided roof)
This building contains the remains of a glass furnace of a type introduced into Britain in the 16thC. It was removed from Rosedale in 1970.

The Crofters Cottage *(right of Glass Furnace)*
This type of simple cottage with a hip-ended thatch was used by crofters in the 13thC. It provided accommodation for the family and their livestock and had an open hearth but no internal walls or chimney.

The Manor House *(left of maypole)*
This large cruck framed building (Page 121) was lived in by the Lord of the Manor of Harome who also used it as his court. It was built in the 16thC for the Morritt family and moved to the museum in 1971.

The Helm Shed
(narrow building right of maypole)
This was used to shelter livestock and consisted of timber posts and a thatch. The posts supported another floor which was used to store corn and beans.

The Harome Cottage *(below the Helm Shed)*
This development of the Crofters Cottage has had "Yorkshire sash windows" added. It was removed from Harome in 1972.

The Cruck House *(bottom building)*
This is a typical yeoman's dwelling of similar construction to Spout House (Page 104). Its cross passage has an exterior door at each end and was used as a threshing area.

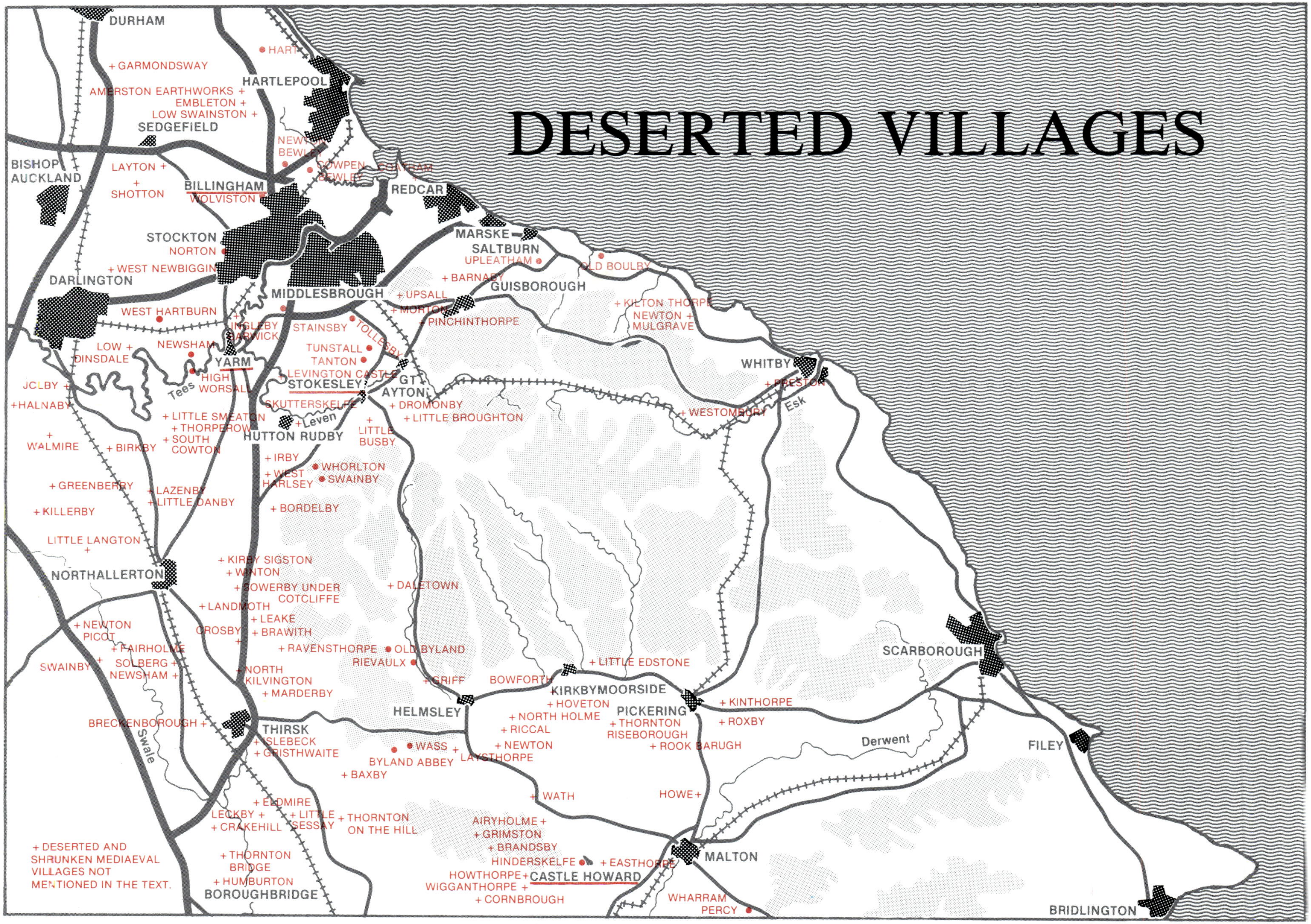
DESERTED VILLAGES
DURHAM
HART
GARMONDSWAY
HARTLEPOOL
AMERSTON EARTHWORKS
EMBLETON
LOW SWAINSTON
SEDGEFIELD
NEWTON BEWLEY
BISHOP AUCKLAND
LAYTON
COWPEN BEWLEY
COATHAM
SHOTTON
BILLINGHAM
WOLVISTON
REDCAR
STOCKTON
NORTON
MARSKE
SALTBURN
UPLEATHAM
OLD BOULBY
WEST NEWBIGGIN
BARNABY
DARLINGTON
GUISBOROUGH
MIDDLESBROUGH
UPSALL
MORTON
KILTON THORPE
NEWTON
MULGRAVE
WEST HARTBURN
PINCHINTHORPE
INGLEBY BARWICK
STAINSBY
TOLLESBY
LOW DINSDALE
NEWSHAM
TUNSTALL
TANTON
YARM
WHITBY
LEVINGTON CASTLE
GT AYTON
PRESTON
JOLBY
HIGH WORSALL
Tees
STOKESLEY
HALNABY
SKUTTERSKELFE
DROMONBY
WESTONBURY
Esk
LITTLE SMEATON
Leven
LITTLE BROUGHTON
THORPEROW
HUTTON RUDBY
LITTLE BUSBY
WALMIRE
BIRKBY
SOUTH COWTON
IRBY
WHORLTON
WEST HARLSEY
SWAINBY
GREENBERRY
LAZENBY
LITTLE DANBY
KILLERBY
BORDELBY
LITTLE LANGTON
KIRBY SIGSTON
WINTON
NORTHALLERTON
SOWERBY UNDER COTCLIFFE
DALETOWN
LANDMOTH
NEWTON PICOT
LEAKE
CROSBY
BRAWITH
FAIRHOLME
RAVENSTHORPE
OLD BYLAND
SCARBOROUGH
SOLBERG
RIEVAULX
LITTLE EDSTONE
SWAINBY
NEWSHAM
NORTH KILVINGTON
GRIFF
BOWFORTH
MARDERBY
KIRKBYMOORSIDE
HOVETON
PICKERING
KINTHORPE
HELMSLEY
NORTH HOLME
THORNTON RISEBOROUGH
RICCAL
ROXBY
BRECKENBOROUGH
THIRSK
ISLEBECK
WASS
NEWTON
ROOK BARUGH
Derwent
FILEY
Swale
GRISTHWAITE
LAYSTHORPE
BYLAND ABBEY
BAXBY
WATH
HOWE
ELDMIRE
LECKBY
LITTLE SESSAY
THORNTON ON THE HILL
AIRYHOLME
CRAKEHILL
GRIMSTON
BRANDSBY
DESERTED AND SHRUNKEN MEDIAEVAL VILLAGES NOT MENTIONED IN THE TEXT.
THORNTON BRIDGE
HINDERSKELFE
EASTHORPE
MALTON
HOWTHORPE
CASTLE HOWARD
HUMBURTON
WIGGANTHORPE
WHARRAM PERCY
BOROUGHBRIDGE
CORNBROUGH
BRIDLINGTON

CHAPTER IX

Prehistoric	Bronze Age	Iron Age	Romans	Danes	Middle Ages	Modern

DESERTED VILLAGES

Holy Cross Church Whorlton

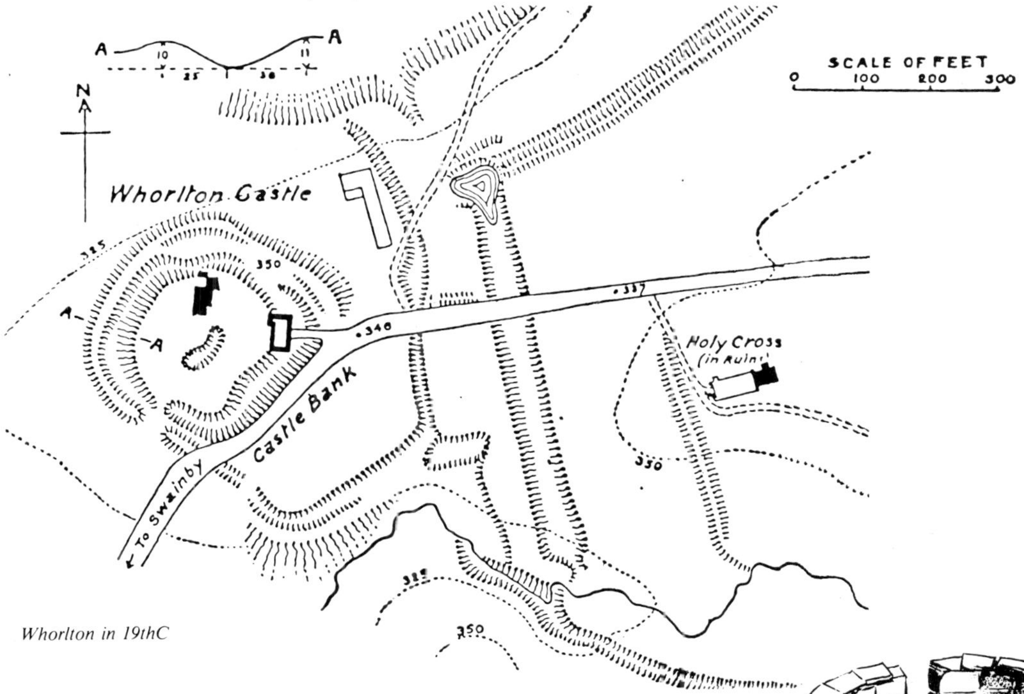

Whorlton in 19thC

There are at least 2500 deserted villages in England and probably another 500 waiting to be discovered. Strictly speaking a deserted mediaeval village — DMV for short — has been totally deserted, but a single farmhouse so often remains that the term still applies. Partly deserted villages are called shrunken villages.

Abandoned well

Until the country was surveyed from the air these sites were thought to be rare. Although we now know that they are common, very few have been discovered in Lancashire and Middlesex, and this can be probably be put down to the thoroughness of modern ploughing methods.

The most obvious characteristics of the DMV are the walls, which having collapsed and been overgrown, appear as grass covered mounds or earthworks. Such earthworks are usually shaped as a rectangle on which houses used to stand, and the resulting raised platforms are known as tofts. The adjoining strips of land behind the tofts were used by the householder as pasture or vegetable plots and are known as crofts. The roads between the tofts are lower than the surrouding land and are called holloways. They have been worn away by centuries of feet and weather — and possibly the over-zealous removal of dung.

Deserted villages cover a number of acres and the painstaking analysis — called for by modern excavation methods — is very expensive. As a result only a few sites have been fully excavated and the best known of these are Wharram Percy on the Yorkshire Wolds and Hound Tor on the granite uplands of Dartmoor.

Many sites in the area covered by this book have been surveyed and a few have been excavated in their most promising parts. But, as a result of excavations carried out at Wharram Percy and elsewhere, we can be tolerably certain of the general reasons for desertion — if not the particular reason in individual cases.

The most common reason for the ultimate desertion of a village was the landowner's decision to give up labour intensive arable farming in favour of sheep — which only needed a few shepherds. But there were often contributing reasons and one of these was the weather. From the time of the Conquest better farming methods coincided with a significant improvement in the weather. As a result marginal land and heavy clay soils were put under the plough and villages were built to be near this land. However, in the 13thC, the weather started to deteriorate and many villages — we know that Hound Tor was one — were gradually abandoned. Even the monastic orders aided the process of desertion. When the Cistercians were at their original site near Rievaulx they moved the inhabitants of a village to Old Byland. The 'old' was an addition to differentiate the village from the later site near Wass. The Benedictines gave the name Beaulieu to Cowpen Bewley and Newton Bewley, which they developed for the benefit of their layworkers at the grange.

Another subsidiary reason for desertion was the Black Death of 1348. This was the worst of a series of plagues which regularly depleted the population until the 17thC. The most common form — the bubonic plague — was transmitted by fleas from the black rat which caused a fever, appalling pain and rapid death. The disease attacked the 'bulboes' — lymphatic glands — causing them to swell and turn black. Billingham, Wolviston, Cowpen Bewley and Norton were all badly affected by the plague.

The Deserted Village of Stainsby

The buildings at the far side of these fascinating earthworks near Thornaby are Stainsby Grange Farm, and the stream beyond is Stainsby Beck. The village was mentioned in the Domesday Survey of 1086. The name means Steinn's hamlet and suggests a Pre-Conquest Scandinavian settlement.

In 1247 Guisborough Priory and Byland Abbey were recorded as having an interest in the fishery, which was probably associated with the bar of land seen alongside the stream — middle right.

Saxton's map of 1577 and Speed's map of 1610 indicate a church at Stainsby but no remains have been found.

The 'tramlines' running parallel to the foot bridge have been identified as the track from Stainton to Thornaby which was in use in 1849. The holloway — just below this track — ran into the village green around which the remains of well planned cottages and crofts can be seen.

The site was deserted by 1757, and about this time the trend was away from arable farming towards sheep farming so that Stainsby may have been a victim of enclosure.

The dual carriageway along the bottom of the photograph is the A19 from Thirsk to Middlesbrough. In 1969 it became the first major road in Britain to be re-directed around a deserted mediaeval village.

Although the plague often caused a village to be abandoned — this was usually only temporary. We know this applied to Cubbington in Buckinghamshire. However over the centuries the plague may have reduced the population of England by as much as half, and this must have contributed to the desertion of many villages.

Some mediaeval villages — which survived the ravages of plague, weather and agriculturists — fell to the hands of 18thC and 19thC landowners. Landowners who built great houses often 'emparked' the surrounding countryside. This happened in Norfolk — where the village of Houghton was rebuilt on the present site of New Houghton and at Castle Howard where the village of Henderskelfe was removed.

There are many sites of DMV's in the Cleveland area. Of those which have been partly excavated like Newsham, West Hartburn, Hart, Tollesby and Old Boulby the dominant reason for desertion appears to have been enclosure for sheep farming in the 16thC.

These deserted villages have nothing to offer the treasure hunter but when they come to be fully excavated their moats, fishponds and windmills, and their kilns, dovecots and potteries will prove to be more fascinating — to the addict — than the intrigues of any soap opera.

Whorlton

This Domesday village on Whorl Hill is more accurately termed a shrunken village rather than a deserted one. It stands just outside Swainby on the Stokesley road to the Tontine Inn and few villages have more to show from the air:

1stC AD — Possible Roman marching camp See Page 50.	*Beyond the church.*
1st-4thC — 150 Roman silver coins found in 1910 and Roman pottery found at various times	*On Whorl Hill.*
11thC — Church of the Holy Cross	*Top right.*
12thC — Motte & bailey built by Robert de Meynell	*Top left*
14thC — Gatehouse of the castle. See Page 81	*Top left.*
11thC-15thC — Tofts and holloway	*Bottom right.*
14thC-15thC — Deerpark dykes	*Below castle and church.*
14thC-15thC — Fishpond	*Between castle and church.*

If Whorlton had grown like other villages these earthworks would have been obscured — but it shrank — and its past was exposed.

Tanton *Bottom left*

This hamlet on the river Tame north of Stokesley was a victim of enclosure, and when the new field boundaries were drawn one of them cut right across the old tofts and holloway.

The white building at the top of the photograph is Tanton Hall which fits so comfortably into the mediaeval street plan that it probably occupies the site of the old manor house.

Upleatham *Bottom right*

This well known church on the Guisborough road to Saltburn marks the position of the original village of Upleatham.

Fragments of an Anglian cross found here suggest that a Christian community existed on this site in Anglo-Saxon times.

The last service was held here in 1836 and since then the church's history has been one of neglect and decay. Its smallness is due to the progressive robbing of its stone.

High Worsall *Top left*

This village may have preceded Yarm as the lowest crossing point of the Tees, and there may once have been a Roman ford here.

The farm, churchyard and tofts are all that remain of the village but 180 years ago the incumbent of the chapel was the Rev. John Graves who wrote the first "History of Cleveland". He recorded that although the village was shrinking nine farm-houses and two cottages remained.

Tunstall *Top right*

Tunstall farm and cottage are the only buildings which survive from the Domesday village of "Tonnestale" north of Stokesley.

In its heyday it was quite a large village and the remains of two fishponds, three wells and the foundations of what may have been a windmill can still be seen.

The ridge and furrow above the fishpond at the top indicates how a "bow" developed when a ploughing team of unweildy oxen began their turn.

VILLAGE FRAMEWORKS

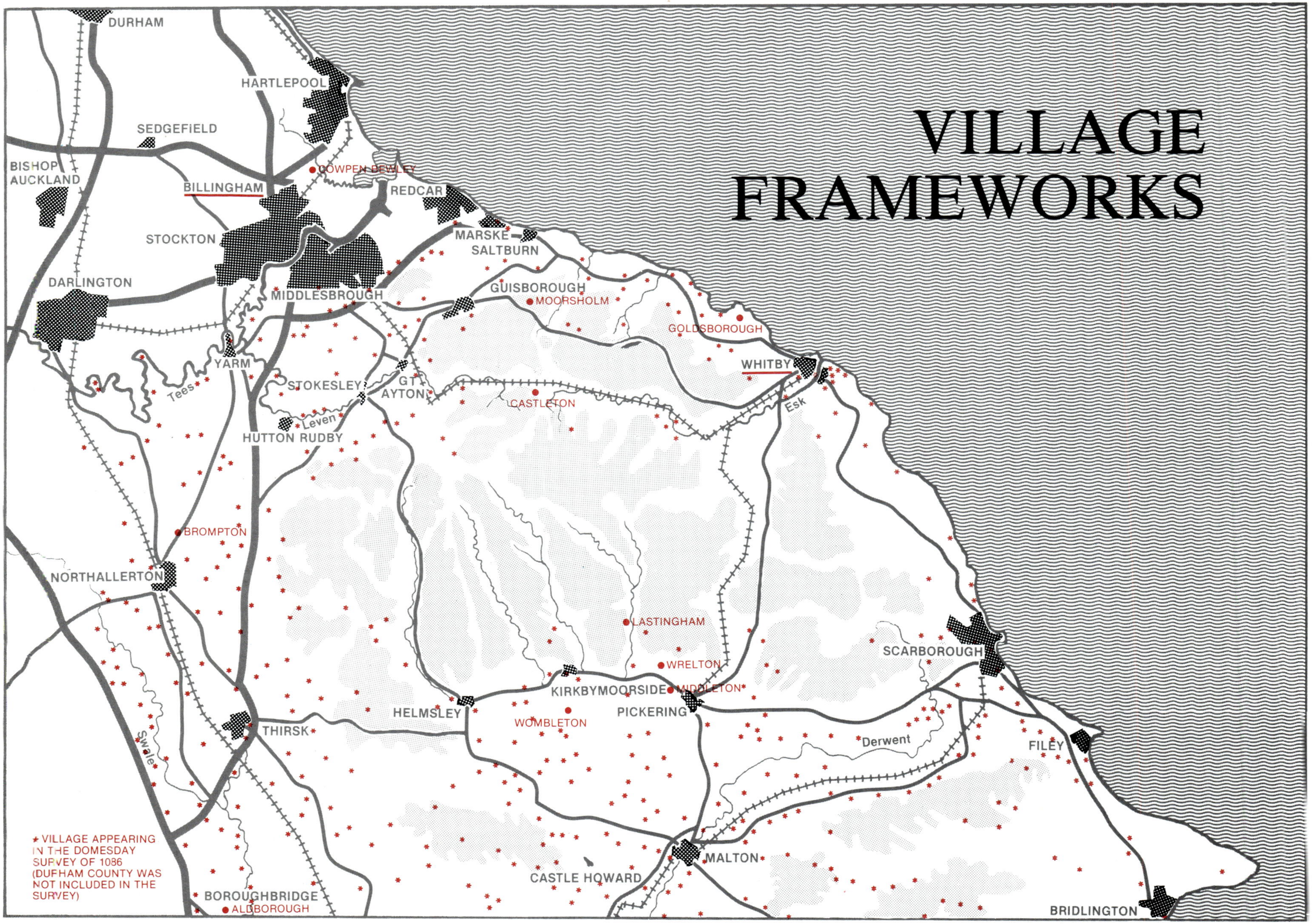

CHAPTER X

Prehistoric	Bronze Age	Iron Age	Romans	Danes	Middle Ages	Modern

THE FRAMEWORK OF VILLAGES

Cruck frame of the Manor House, Ryedale Folk Museum

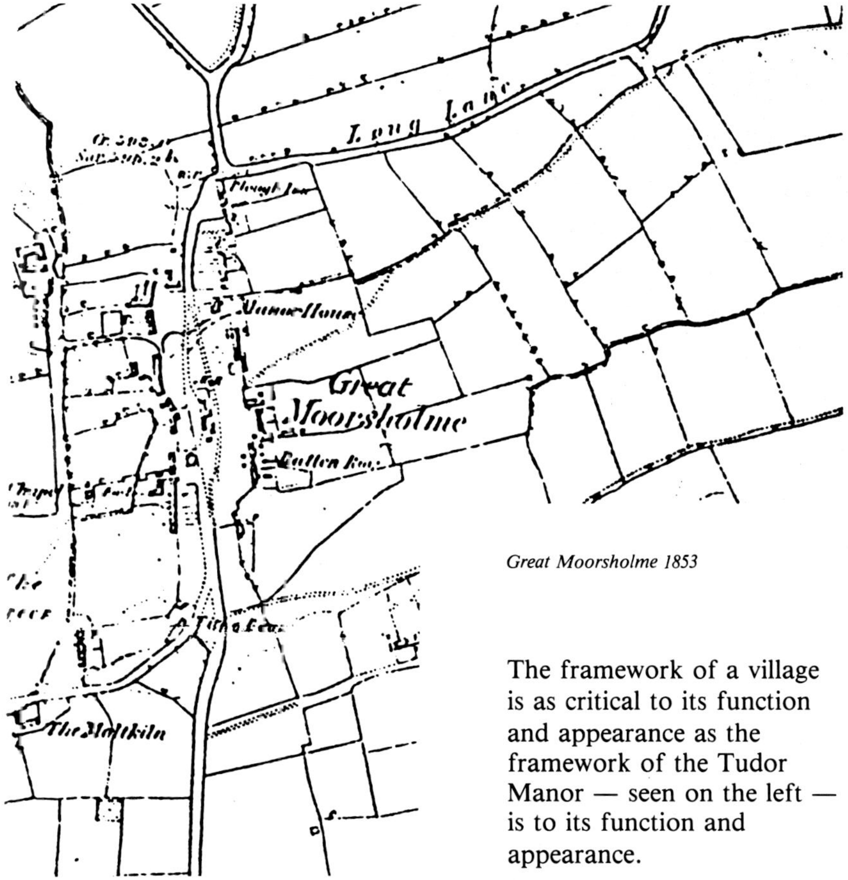

Great Moorsholme 1853

The framework of a village is as critical to its function and appearance as the framework of the Tudor Manor — seen on the left — is to its function and appearance.

In the Middle Ages nearly all work was agricultural and as a result most people lived in villages near the fields. As the majority of the villages and towns in which we live today were founded at that time the types of framework — or plan — adopted have had far reaching consequences for us all.

The best way to uncover this framework is to study the large scale maps made by Ordnance Survey in 1856 which can be found in most county archives or libraries. These maps are referred to in the commentaries on the photographs in this chapter because they provide a last glimpse of our mediaeval villages before many of them disappeared beneath the urban sprawl of the Victorian period.

Village frameworks are of two different types: rows and agglomerates. Either type can be planned but whether they **should** be planned seems to have been as much a matter of opinion for Anglo-Saxon and Norman landowners as it is for us. If a formal plan was adopted — and it turned out to be wrong for the needs of the community — the consquences were more serious than if the village had been allowed to develop naturally.

Rapid change however was unusual in mediaeval times and many landowners opted for a formal plan. Sometimes formality was necessary for reasons of defence, and many towns developed from mediaeval castle baileys, and even Roman marching camps like Aldborough (Page 125).

Cowpen Bewley — opposite — and Moorsholm (Page 125) are typical planned mediaeval villages whereas Whitby (Page 127) and Goldsborough (Page 129) are typical of the sort of community which developed naturally. Both types have their advocates and detractors but on social and aesthetic grounds, villages which merely straggle along existing highways like Castleton (Page 129), have less to commend them than agglomerates which usually have a focal point. Whitby is a good example of a community which faced serious geographical constraints. It was trapped between a cliff and a river, but it was so important to remain near both, that these constraints moulded its distinctive appearance.

One of the most obvious elements of a planned mediaeval village is a green. Cowpen Bewley has such a green and the houses served to enclose this common pasture. However aerial photography and early maps indicate that there were many other elements in these villages such as short or long tofts, short or long crofts, central churches or off centre churches, rectangular churchyards or oval churchyards. Even the greens varied: they could be rectangular like Cowpen Bewley or square like Aldborough. Moorsholm seems to have an irregular, partly enclosed green. The apparent green in the centre of Goldsborough is a private field which has remained hedged after buildings were removed. As such this site indicates shrinkage which, if continued, can lead to desertion (Chapter IX). The green in an apparently unplanned village like Wrelton (Page 129) has developed to meet the need for extra space at a busy intersection.

Cowpen Bewley

This is a particularly good example of a planned mediaeval village. It lies only a mile to the north of the vast chemical works of ICI's Agricultural Division at Billingham.

Cowpen Bewley was, from the start, intended to be a village with common grazing land in the centre. Nowadays we regard a green as a visual amenity but that would have been the last consideration of a Lord of the Manor in the Middle Ages.

As in most planned villages — the crofts behind each cottage are of equal length. Access to the back of the crofts, and to the outfields, was via the back lanes. Although the back lanes in this village have not been used for hundreds of years there can be no doubt where they used to lie.

Unlike many villages of this kind Cowpen Bewley has not become a smart dormitory adjunct to the nearby works, but has retained its farm buildings and farm workers houses facing the green.

Conservationists have preserved and renovated the five sided wheelhouse — just below the centre of the photograph. This was the building in which horses drove the village mill-wheels in the days before steam power.

Although it is a new science, the study of these elements in village plans is very enlightening. A better understanding of these elements may make it easier to date the foundation of a village and detect those factors which lead to shrinkage or expansion. Although there are a limited number of elements, the way they have combined has produced something which we all recognise as distinctly English, and different from villages on the Continent.

Even the exceptions to this distinctiveness are significant. Some villages in the north of England bear more than a passing resemblance to villages in Germany and Scandinavia and it is from these villages that our Anglo-Saxon and Viking ancestors came.

These same elements may also have social implications and a study of successful combinations may be of interest to modern planners. The ribbon development — which was rife between the wars — might never have happened if we had known more about mediaeval linear villages.

Research at Durham University has demonstrated the different ways in which these elements combine together in different parts of the country. Such information might be of use to archaeologists when the study has been extended over the whole country. The symbols at the end of this chapter have been proposed as the "bricks" from which a comprehensive collection of county maps could be built.

Domesday Villages

The Domesday Survey of England south of the river Tees was completed precisely 900 years before this aerial survey of ancient Cleveland.

The Norman survey was based upon — and frequently compared to — the earlier survey carried out by Edward the Confessor. Most of the villages in the North and East Ridings had been laid waste twenty years before, and the King's surveyors found it difficult to communicate with the few Anglo-Saxons whom they found hiding in the ruins of the villages. As a result the surveyors interpreted many of the names in a Latin or French manner. In spite of this, and in spite of the harrying, most of the villages can still be identified. Some were deserted in mediaeval times but the majority have provided the framework of the towns and villages we know today. These Domesday villages are shown on the map at the beginning of this chapter.

Planned Villages

Brompton *Bottom left*

This is the northern part of Brompton near Northallerton illustrated on Page 55. It is a good example of a planned village with a green and a stream.

Since the Ordnance Survey in 1856 this part of Brompton has not undergone any major changes. The road bridge — bottom left — used to be a footbridge and ford, some houses have been rebuilt and some wooden sheds have been turned into garages, but the number of houses has remained the same.

Aldborough *Bottom right*

This small town near Boroughbridge was not planned by an Anglo-Saxon or a Norman landowner but by a Roman General in the 1stC AD.

The plan on Page 46 shows that the walls followed the edges of the photograph, except the right hand edge which was a Roman road joining the east and west gates. The top of the two parallel roads was also a Roman road leading to the south gate on the left.

The other roads and the green were of much later construction, but even the mediaeval crofts were limited by the foundations of the Roman walls.

Moorsholm *Top left*

The Ordnance Survey Map of 1856 does not make it clear if this planned village — which lies four miles east of Guisborough — ever had a traditional green. At that time the green was a field — top right — which has remained communal property by becoming a playing field.

The buildings of the village have changed their use, but the only significant additions during the last 130 years have been the houses running along the top of the photograph, and the farm buildings — centre right.

Wombleton *Top right*

This is a classic linear village without a green, but with well defined back lanes, known as Backside Lane and Pass Lane. Since its foundation there seems to have been a minimum of infill building but there has been one big change — a small modern estate on the right of the photograph.

The plan of this estate bears a striking resemblance to the original plan of the village.

✱	*Regular Radial*
▬	*Regular Row*
▪ ▪ ▪	*Irregular Row*
▪ ▪ ▪	*Agglomeration*
#	*Regular Grid*
●	*Irregular Agglomeration*

Whitby

"Whitby" is Old Norse for "the settlement of a man called Hwite" but it is also possible that this fishing village is named after the cliffs which — although not white — are light in colour.

The original village was probably founded earlier than St. Hilda's monastery of 657 AD, and earlier than the Roman watch tower on the top of the cliff, which was referred to by the Venerable Bede.

Although no evidence has been found it seems likely that early man settled on the beach below the cliff. The sea and the river Esk would have provided him with food and the cliffs would have provided protection.

At whatever date the village was founded the lack of flat ground dictated that the settlement grew in a haphazard manner — without planning or form. The cliffs and the sea restricted expansion which could only take place in one direction — along the river bank.

Anglo-Saxon rubbish from the monastery — apparently thrown over the cliff edge — has been recovered from the back-yards of the houses below.

Whitby must have been an efficient economic unit, but its charm and good looks are the result of man's failure to make it look like one.

Castleton *Bottom left*

A village was bound to develop at this meeting point of five dales in the northern half of the moors.

The castle which stood on the wooded mound — centre right — was probably built to dominate the road. The Ordnance Survey Map of 1856 suggests that the castle had a bailey — by the shape of the fields to the left of the motte.

The modern developments at the top of the photograph, and on the left of the motte, contrast with the unplanned nature of the rest of the village.

Goldsborough *Bottom right*

The suffix "borough" is not a reliable guide to Roman origins, but in this case the foundation of the village may have some connection with the Roman signal station half a mile to the east (Page 51).

The village appears to have grown up at a point where two roads met and where the needs of the two farmhouses called for some extra buildings. The aerial indications are that Goldsborough never needed anything more than this.

Lastingham *Top left*

This site was chosen by the monks of St. Cedd because it was remote, because it had a water supply and because it was a gift from the local landowner.

A number of villages were carefully planned by monks but Lastingham was not one of them. It was allowed to develop naturally around the monastery buildings — which used to stand in the field seen centre left.

Wrelton *Top right*

Judging by the "ton" suffix this village — like Middleton a mile to the east — was probably founded between the departure of the Romans and the arrival of the Normans.

However a Roman marching camp may have stood here before that and there is a faint suggestion of such a shape in the photograph.

Notwithstanding this, the village has many of the hallmarks of a village which grew from the embryo of two farm houses on the opposite side of a 'T' junction. The road on the right is a modern by-pass.

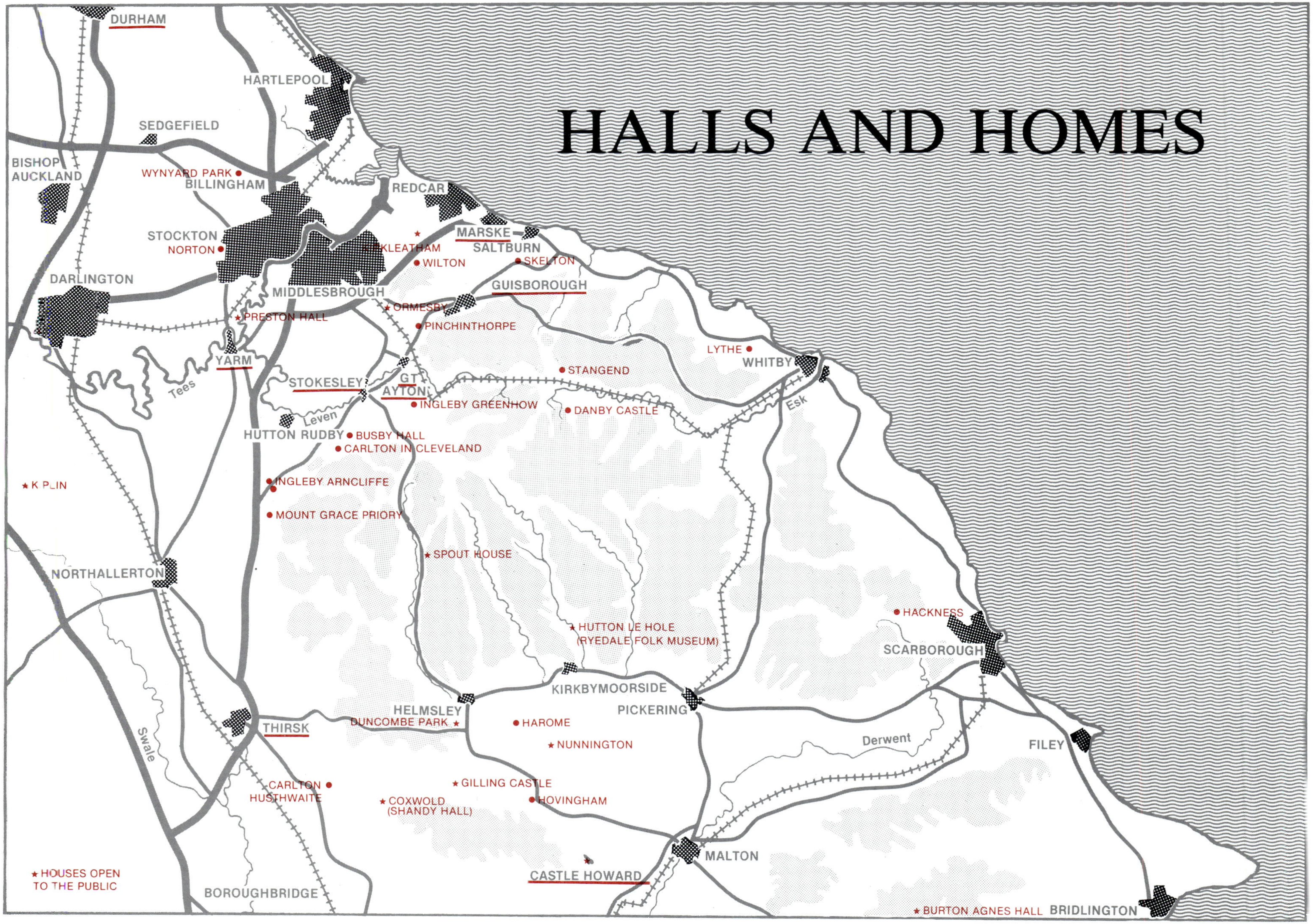
HALLS AND HOMES
DURHAM
HARTLEPOOL
SEDGEFIELD
BISHOP AUCKLAND
WYNYARD PARK
BILLINGHAM
REDCAR
STOCKTON
NORTON
MARSKE
SALTBURN
KIRKLEATHAM
WILTON
SKELTON
DARLINGTON
MIDDLESBROUGH
GUISBOROUGH
ORMESBY
PRESTON HALL
PINCHINTHORPE
LYTHE
WHITBY
YARM
STANGEND
STOKESLEY
GT AYTON
INGLEBY GREENHOW
DANBY CASTLE
Tees
Leven
Esk
HUTTON RUDBY
BUSBY HALL
CARLTON IN CLEVELAND
INGLEBY ARNCLIFFE
MOUNT GRACE PRIORY
SPOUT HOUSE
NORTHALLERTON
HACKNESS
HUTTON LE HOLE (RYEDALE FOLK MUSEUM)
SCARBOROUGH
KIRKBYMOORSIDE
HELMSLEY
PICKERING
DUNCOMBE PARK
HAROME
THIRSK
NUNNINGTON
Swale
Derwent
FILEY
CARLTON HUSTHWAITE
GILLING CASTLE
COXWOLD (SHANDY HALL)
HOVINGHAM
MALTON
HOUSES OPEN TO THE PUBLIC
CASTLE HOWARD
BOROUGHBRIDGE
BURTON AGNES HALL
BRIDLINGTON

CHAPTER XI

Prehistoric	Bronze Age	Iron Age	Romans	Danes	Middle Ages	Modern

HALLS AND HOMES

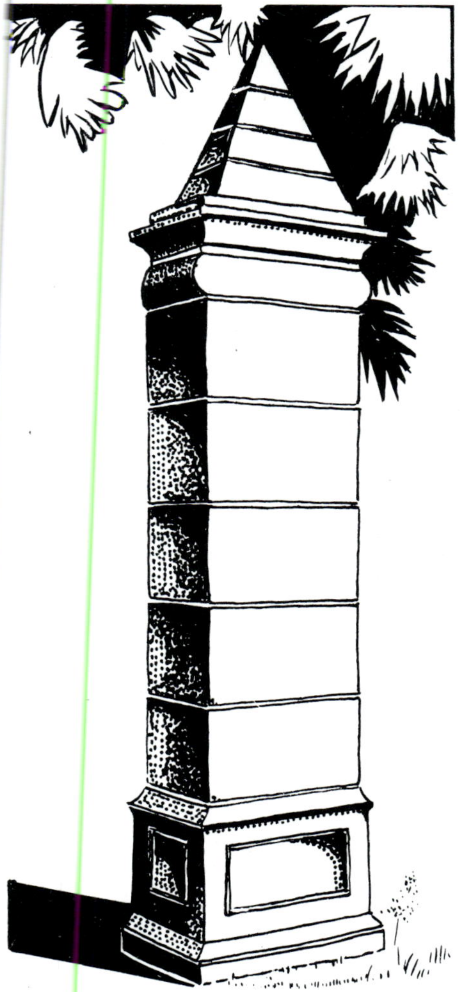

Gate pillar, Pinchinthorpe Hall

Sir William Turner's Hospital, Kirkleatham

The theory that history consists of an unbroken series of advances towards excellence is nowhere more easily discredited than in the field of housing. We know that the Romans built villas in the area to a high standard of heating, sanitation and comfort but during the Dark Ages the skills and materials necessary to achieve this standard were lost. In fact Anglo-Saxon settlers avoided Roman sites whenever they could.

Marske Hall

Although no remains of Anglo-Saxon houses have been found in the area we can assume that there were many of the "pit and two post" type. These were thatched wooden huts and it was once thought that the bottom of the pit formed the floor. It is now believed that the floors were raised and made of wood which has since rotted away.

Mediaeval Houses

During the harrying of the north most wooden houses were burnt to the ground. As the Norman domination of the area depended on stone castles, more quarries came into use than at any time since the Romans. The growth of monasteries and the rebuilding of churches in stone ensured that stone was available for other building projects.

However crofters and yeoman farmers lived in single-storey thatched cottages with cob walls. Excellent examples of these cottages have been built in the Ryedale Folk Museum at Hutton-le-Hole (Page 111), but there is another, in its orignial location, called Spout House in Bilsdale (Page 104).

Bigger and better houses of two stories were made of longer timbers with stone flags for the floors and shingles for the roof. A manor house of this type was removed from Harome near Helmsley to the Ryedale Folk Museum in 1971.

The best examples of half-timbered houses which are still lived in, are in Lavenham, Chester and Shakespeare country but the only one in the Cleveland area is a thatched cottage in Carlton Husthwaite (page 138).

Early in the Middle Ages a castle was always a home and there are still a number of castles in the area which are used as homes. Durham Castle (Page 93) is occupied by students of the University, Danby Castle is a farm house and Gilling Castle is lived in by prep. school boys.

Stone did not become the building material for houses of lesser lords, squires and priests until the 12thC. There is evidence that the stone house in Ingleby Arncliffe (Page 103) could be the same as the "Priest's House" which stood in the village in 1300. The Old Hall of Burton Agnes Hall — now the laundry — is the only stone house which goes as far back as the 12thC.

Elizabethan and Jacobean Halls

The main part of Burton Agnes Hall was built in 1601 by which time a number of stone halls were being built. Some of these — like Ingleby Manor (Page 135) at Ingleby Greenhow and Kiplin Hall, near Catterick — which was built for Lord Baltimore the founder of Maryland — were of the fortified type. Most halls at this time reflect the Renaissance taste for classical round arches rather than the gothic pointed kind which had been perfected in church architecture. Nunnington Hall near Helmsley, the priorhouse of Mount Grace Priory (Page 89) and Marske Hall near Redcar (now a Cheshire Home) all belong to this period.

Castle Howard

On the southern edge of the area covered by this book lies this most magnificent of 17thC country houses.

Henderskelfe Castle stood on this site for several hundred years and some of its bailey walls can still be seen. It was burnt down in 1693 and Charles Howard — the third Earl of Carlisle — commissioned Vanbrugh to build a mansion in its place.

Charles Vanbrugh was a young and successful playwright who had never designed a building of any kind. His collaborator was Nicholas Hawksmoor who was Christopher Wren's Clerk of Works. Together they adopted the classical style on a grand scale and became the first architects to incorporate a "dome and lantern" in a private house.

The formal gardens in the foreground were laid out on ground previously occupied by the village of Henderskelfe.

The last owner was Mr. George Howard who was Chairman of the Governors of the BBC and became Lord Howard of Henderskelfe in 1983.

Georgian Halls

By the Georgian period the prime considerations in the design of a house were convenience and good proportion. The great halls of manor houses — which had been the social, legal and military centres of their areas — became hallways. Some castles, like Castle Howard and Skelton Castle, became Georgian halls in appearance if not in name.

Castle Howard (page 133) is without doubt the most original and magnificent home in the area. It was designed by Vanbrugh when Henderskelfe Castle was burnt down in 1693. Vanbrugh is also thought to have had a hand in Duncombe Park (Page 136) and these two houses exemplify the symmetry and surface decoration which were such important elements in Georgian architecture. The effect is most obvious in the massive wings and classical columns of palladian mansions, but it can also be seen in diminutive versions like Carlton Manor in Carlton-in-Cleveland near Stokesley. Among the best examples in the area are Hackness Hall, Arncliffe Hall near Ingleby Arncliffe and the Old Hall at Kirkleatham (Page 141) — built as a Free School in 1709.

The same symmetrical effect was probably intended by Sir Thomas Worsley — the Surveyor General — when he built Hovingham Hall (page 63), but only one of the two wings which he planned was built. It was also intended at Mulgrave Castle (Page 139) at Lythe by the Duchess of Buckingham but that was before the gothic revival. A later owner attempted to achieve a more romantic appearance by adding two gothic towers and a wing. Skelton Castle (Page 83) was intended to be gothic from the outset — as was Wilton Castle — the ICI centre near Redcar — which was built about 1807. But whereas Skelton Castle is intentionally asymmetrical, Wilton Castle attempted to be both symmetrical **and** romantic.

The most common type of Georgian Hall was built for the squire, parson and successful farmer. They were built in fine ashlar stone and the smaller ones have adapted well to modern living. The terrace houses built in this period are responsible for the delightful appearance of many Cleveland high streets such as Stokesley, Norton, Guisborough, Yarm and Thirsk.

This brief review of old houses in the area has had to omit many beautiful and interesting buildings especially Georgian and Victorian ones. However most of the houses, which are open to the public are shown on the map at the beginning of the chapter.

Ingleby Manor — Ingleby Greenhow

This 16thC building can claim to be the oldest manor house in the area. By the time of the Tudors, castles had become indefensible due to the invention of cannons which could batter their walls down from a safe distance. As a result important buildings were constructed around a courtyard — with a token tower above its entrance.

Ingleby Manor has such a courtyard — now divided into two by a central hall — and a Renaissance arcade of round classical arches rather than pointed gothic ones.

The Eures were Lords of the Manor of Ingleby until 1608 when Sir David Foulis bought Ingleby from them. It remained in the Foulis family until 1850 when it passed — through the female line — to the Sidneys of Penshurst in Kent. Viscount De L'Isle K.G., V.C., of that family, still retains an interest in the Norman Church of St. Andrews at the end of the drive.

The original tower above the entrance to the courtyard — on the left — was reduced in height when the house was altered in the 19thC. Some fine Tudor windows in the front were removed at the same time.

Ingleby Manor is still a private house but when the Sidneys sold it in 1950 it was divided into residential apartments.

Duncombe Park

Duncombe Park, which is owned by Lord Feversham, is an imposing 18thC hall with magnificent grounds landscaped in the grand manner.

Sir Charles Duncombe — who bought the estate in 1689 — was a city banker and Lord Mayor of London in 1708.

The house was designed in 1711 by William Wakefield who it is believed collaborated with Vanbrugh — the designer of Castle Howard (Page 133). The two wings were added by Sir Charles Barry in 1843, but in 1879 the main building — with the exception of the facade — was destroyed by fire and the interior was reconstructed to a design by William Young.

The superb views down to the Rye Valley and Rievaulx have — until recently — been enjoyed by the pupils of a girls boarding school.

Wynyard Park →

Situated just a mile to the west of Billingham this magnificent Victorian mansion was built by the third Marquis of Londonderry following the destruction of an earlier house by fire in 1839.

The extensive parklands and artificial lake made an ideal setting for Philip Wyatt's neo-classical design. The best external feature is the entrance portico with its Corinthian columns — seen in the photograph. Inside, the statue gallery — with its octagonal centrepiece and clusters of marble columns — provides an elegant setting which is not to be found elsewhere in the County of Cleveland.

Carlton Husthwaite

Carlton Husthwaite once consisted of two mediaeval villages — Carlton and Husthwaite. It has a mediaeval church which is furnished with fine Jacobean pews and pulpit — and it had this thatched cottage.

This building is a half-timbered manor house of the kind so often found in Shakespeare country and East Anglia — but it is the only authentic "black and white" house in the Cleveland area.

Its construction is similar to the Manor House at the Ryedale Folk Museum which once stood in Harome. The cob walls of the original Harome Manor were made of a mixture of clay, sand, straw and gravel, but the bays between the crucks of ***this*** *manor were sub-divided by timbers and the spaces filled with wattle and daub. Wattle is a mesh of thin laths or branches, and daub is mud or clay mixed with horsehair.*

The roof is hip-end thatched which means that the gable ends are also thatched. This construction method gives the wind less chance of lifting the roof.

Mulgrave Castle

This impressive 18thC house near Lythe was built for Catherine Duchess of Buckingham — the daughter of James II.

The wings were added by Sir John Soane in the 1780's and the fine grounds were laid out by Humphry Repton in 1792. In the early 1800's, the gothic towers, the west wing and the castellations were added with the object of reducing the symmetry of the house and achieving a "romantic" appearance.

It is the home of the Marquis of Normanby — the Lord Lieutenant of North Yorkshire. Mulgrave Castle took its name from the 13thC castle — the ruins of which lie a mile to the west (Page 76).

Ormesby Hall

James Pennyman purchased the Manor of Ormesby in 1600 and started building a Jacobean house shortly afterwards. It was never finished and the Georgian house in the photograph was built by Dorothy Pennnyman in 1745.

Sir George Pennyman — the 6th Baronet — lavishly decorated many of the rooms in the Adam style and constructed the splendid stables to a design by John Carr of York.

The last Pennyman to live in the house was Colonel James Pennyman. He left the property to the National Trust in 1961, but his wife lived there until her death in 1983.

Langbaurgh Hall

This simple 19thC hall — built in a style known locally as Quaker Georgian — is typical of the many sandstone halls built at the end of the Georgian period by Cleveland farmers, who became prosperous by taking advantage of new farming techniques.

The Quaker John Richardson built a tannery next to his farm at Langbaurgh outside Great Ayton, and used the bark from his oaks to cure the hides which local farmers brought to him.

The hall was built in 1834 but the gardens were laid out only 30 years ago by the author's father.

Busby Hall

Typical of the many fine ashlar sandstone halls built by Georgian landowners — Busby Hall south of Stokesley — has the unusual distinction of being lived in by the descendent of the man who built it in 1764. He was Sir George Marwood — High Sheriff of Yorkshire — whose forebears had lived on, or near, the site since Tudor times.

Although the Marwoods have lived here for more than four centuries the magnificent Spanish chestnut seen behind the main body of the house, has been here for a least a century longer.

Sir William Turner's Hospital Kirkleatham

Over 300 years ago this "hospital" was founded to look after twenty poor people. They had to be single, elderly — and half of them had to be women — but they were all provided with excellent living conditions.

After a few years the buildings were reconstructed and the present chapel and library are considered to be the finest examples of 17thC architecture in the area.

Most of the buildings in the photograph were conceived and paid for by one man. William Turner — the second son of his family — went to London as a young man and eventually became an eminent woollen draper. He was knighted in 1662 and became Lord Mayor of London seven years later.

Kirkleatham Old Hall — in the foreground — was built by Cholmley Turner M.P., under the terms of Sir William's will. It was built as a Free School in 1709 and is now a museum for the Borough of Langbaurgh.

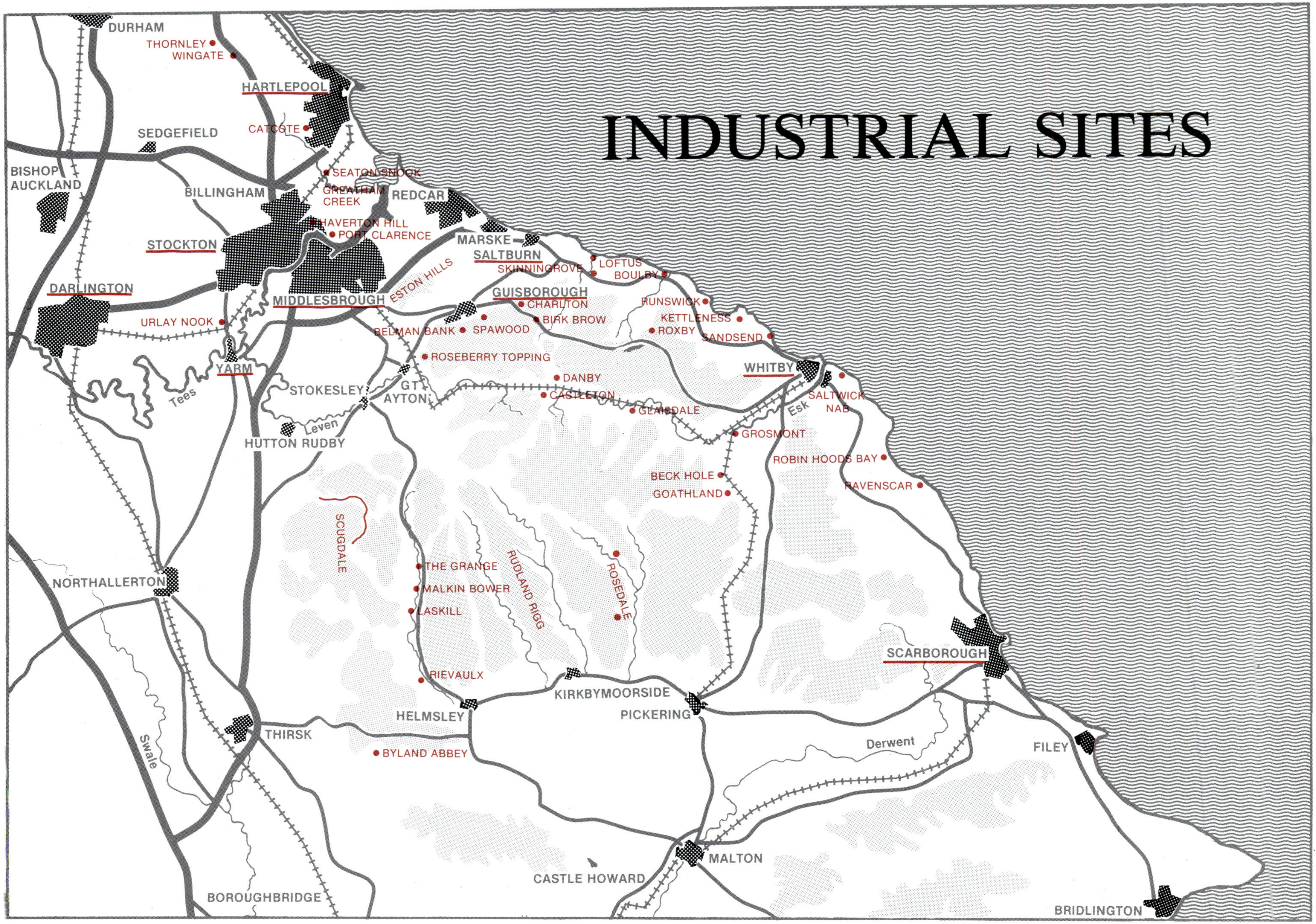
INDUSTRIAL SITES
DURHAM
THORNLEY
WINGATE
HARTLEPOOL
SEDGEFIELD
CATCOTE
BISHOP AUCKLAND
BILLINGHAM
SEATON SNOOK
GREATHAM CREEK
REDCAR
HAVERTON HILL
PORT CLARENCE
MARSKE
STOCKTON
SALTBURN
SKINNINGROVE
LOFTUS
BOULBY
ESTON HILLS
DARLINGTON
MIDDLESBROUGH
GUISBOROUGH
CHARLTON
RUNSWICK
KETTLENESS
URLAY NOOK
BIRK BROW
ROXBY
BELMAN BANK
SPAWOOD
SANDSEND
ROSEBERRY TOPPING
YARM
WHITBY
DANBY
STOKESLEY
GT AYTON
CASTLETON
SALTWICK NAB
Tees
GLAISDALE
Esk
Leven
GROSMONT
HUTTON RUDBY
ROBIN HOODS BAY
BECK HOLE
RAVENSCAR
GOATHLAND
SCUGDALE
THE GRANGE
ROSEDALE
RUDLAND RIGG
NORTHALLERTON
MALKIN BOWER
LASKILL
SCARBOROUGH
RIEVAULX
KIRKBYMOORSIDE
HELMSLEY
PICKERING
Swale
THIRSK
Derwent
FILEY
BYLAND ABBEY
MALTON
CASTLE HOWARD
BOROUGHBRIDGE
BRIDLINGTON

CHAPTER XII

Prehistoric	Bronze Age	Iron Age	Romans	Danes	Middle Ages	Modern

INDUSTRIAL HERITAGE

The Transporter, Middlesbrough

The Hetton Locomotive built by George Stephenson in 1822

Before the Industrial Revolution the area had, at various times, gained a reputation for its jet, alum and salt. However, more commonplace materials have for centuries been quarried for the benefit of builders and farmers. Stone, sand, gravel and whinstone have been used for buildings and roads, and limestone and potash have been used for fertiliser. Gas is a newcomer but has not been extracted since 1974.

Jet

It was jet that first made Cleveland different from other areas. As early as the Bronze Age pieces of jet were collected from the sea shore where they had fallen from the cliffs. They were worked into ornaments and the remains of an elaborate necklace — consisting of 286 separate pieces — has been found in a burial mound on the moors. The Romans also used jet for ornaments which they exported throughout their empire. In mediaeval times it became popular for church ornaments such as crucifixes, but it was not until Victorian times that the demand justified extensive mining. Two mines were opened at the foot of the cliffs at Sandsend and Runswick, and later many dales on the northern and north-western edges of the Cleveland Hills — such as Scugdale (Page 151) — became lined with jet pits. By 1873 the industry employed 1500 people in mining and working the material at Whitby — and in this year a turnover of £90,000 per year was achieved.

Alum

Alum has been used for 4,000 years in the tanning process, and as a mordant for fixing dyes. It is the double sulphate of potassium and aluminium, and the secret of its production was known first to the Arabs, then to the Turks and finally to the Papacy. About 1600 — while the production was still a papal secret — alum was discovered at Belman Bank south of Guisborough and the right to mine it became a crown monopoly. The process was vastly expensive and used up great acreages of woodland for fuel but such was the demand that coal was brought in from Sunderland and Tyneside, and may have been mined on Rudland Rigg (Page 147). The most important alum mines were at Boulby, Loftus, Saltwick Nab, Sandsend Ness and Ravenscar, and many of the headlands on the coast were permanently disfigured by the mining. The last mine to close was at Kettleness (Page 51) in 1871 by which time it had been discovered that alum could be made more cheaply from colliery shale.

Salt

The mouth of the Tees has probably satisfied a local demand for salt from prehistoric times. In the Middle Ages much of Greatham Creek (Page 107) was used to process it. Coal from Hartlepool beach was used to boil salt water in salterns, and the spoil from hundreds of years of this process can still be seen. In 1886 Tennants Saltworks opened and the whole area from Greatham to Haverton Hill was covered in rigs which were used to drill wells and to pump brine to the surface. This method greatly increased production and extensive markets were opened up outside the area. Tennants eventually passed into the hands of Cerebos Salt, but production did not cease until 1970.

Rosedale Ironstone Workings

The most spectacular of all the great Victorian mining ventures in Cleveland can still be seen in Rosedale.

Following the discovery by Bolckow of ironstone on the North York Moors, the most important mines were soon in operation on the northern and eastern edges of the moors. There was a subsidiary area in Rosedale consisting of two mines. The larger lay on the eastern side of the upper dale, and the smaller on the western side further down the dale. The calcining kilns of the western mines can be seen in this photograph.

The Rosedale seams were the least predictable in Cleveland. One seam lying near the surface was of low grade and contained a large proportion of silica. Beneath it lay pockets of high grade ore, and the two grades could easily be blended together.

The railway track running across the top of the photograph was completed in 1861, and the battery of calcining kilns were built at the terminus. Coal and ore were burnt together in these kilns to remove carbonate material and thereby reduce transport costs.

The sandstone facing blocks of these once impressive kilns were removed in the 1950's.

Early Iron Making

Iron was smelted in the Iron Age at Roxby (Page 38) and probably by the Romans at Catcote near Hartlepool. There is no evidence of mediaeval iron making until about 1200 when forges were in operation at Rievaulx and Laskills. Slag has been found at these places and also at The Grange and Malkin Bower nearby. By 1223 a bloomery was in production near Guisborough and a small forge was at work near Danby

Rievaulx continued to be a centre for local iron making until the 17thC. We know that there were French iron workers at a smithy near the abbey in 1538 and that a forge here produced 45 tonnes of iron in that year. A few years later — in 1576 — one of the first blast furnaces in the north of England was opened and began producing 13 hundredweights (.7 tonne) of pig iron per day. Records ceased at Rievaulx in 1647 at which time production probably stopped.

Smaller forges and furnaces operated at Danby and Castleton, and also at Byland Abbey which may account for some of the earthworks in the photograph on page 91. Iron making — like alum making — required large amounts of fuel. When charcoal was used the process had a serious effect on woodlands, although this was mitigated by the practice of coppicing.

The Industrial Revolution

Blast furnaces were in operation on the Wear and Tyne before the Tees. Ironstone nodules — from the beaches at Robin Hoods Bay, Saltburn and Scarborough — were being sent to the Wear as early as 1745. By 1820 open cast mining had started in Saltburn and Scarborough but the ore was still sent to the Wear. The ore from Wilson's Ironstone Mine at Grosmont — which produced 100,000 tonnes per year — was sent to the Tyne as late as 1836.

All this was known to John Vaughan so we must not imagine that his discovery of a piece of ironstone in the Eston Hills, whilst shooting rabbits, was a total surprise. The full extent of the rich Grosmont seam — which stretched as far as Skinningrove and Guisborough (Page 152) — was not exploited until 1860 but by then the Bolckow and Vaughan works in Middlesbrough were using ironstone from the Eston Hills and Rosedale.

The Beck Hole mine near Goathland was in operation by 1857 and the Glaisdale mine by 1863. Neither lasted for more than a few years, but the ore from such mines was enough to lift the production of pig iron in Middlesbrough to 600,000 tonnes per year.

Bell Pits on Rudland Rigg

The sight of these serried ranks of bell pits — on my first cross country flight in 1983 — kindled my interest in industrial archaeology.

The mining of coal on the North York Moors has been going on for hundreds of years. Until the advent of ventilator pumps in the middle of the last century minerals could only be mined by the sinking of a vertical shaft, enlarging it into a bell shaped chamber, and then tunnelling sideways into lateral corridors. Once a corridor was more than 75ft. (25m) long, the air became foul and a new shaft had to be sunk.

This process accounts for the regularity of the pits seen in the photograph. The centre of each pit is approximately 150ft. (50m) from the next.

From the air the size of a spoil heap is deceptively small, but closer inspection shows each to be the size of a large barn.

The Development of the Tees Valley

Stockton

Long before the rise of Stockton, Yarm was an important mediaeval port exporting agricultural produce to Europe. However in the Georgian period political stability and the enterprise of local people provided the right conditions for rapid growth. Without these conditions the coal and iron industries might have remained matters of local interest only, but in the event Durham coal became a trigger for the Industrial Revolution. The bridge built in Stockton in 1769 made the town the lowest crossing point on the Tees and the natural embarkation point for south Durham coal. Some of the wealth generated from this export business was used in 1810 to prolong the life of the port by the construction of the Mandale Cut. At the inaugural dinner for this event there was talk of a railway from Stockton to Darlington, but this did not materialise until 1825. The inn — where the historic decision was finally taken — can be seen in the photograph on page 101.

The enormous potential of this railway was quickly realised by businessmen such as Robert Wilson, who in 1833 opened his fertilizer and sulphuric acid plant alongside the line at Urlay Nook. In the same year the railway reached Port Clarence which soon became a local coal port. In 1831 Stockton again prolonged the life of the port by constructing the Portrack Cut (Page 153)

West Hartlepool

The railway reached West Hartlepool in 1840 and the West Harbour was completed seven years later. This dock became an efficient coal export point and made riverside coal staithes, such as those at Port Clarence, obsolete. Within five years the Jackson Dock was also exporting coal.

The zinc and acid works at Seaton Snook was constructed in 1906 and this historic lead chamber acid plant was to become the last of its kind in England. It closed in 1970, but spoil from spent oxide can be seen on the site.

Hartlepool Headland

The railway arrived at the ancient headland of Hartlepool (Page 59) **from the north** in 1836, and the Victoria Dock was built within four years. This dock also became a coal exporting point — in this case for the coal from the Thornley and Wingate mines. Hartlepool and West Hartlepool were separated by 200 acres of marshland known as the Slake and their railways did not meet until 1860.

Middlesbrough
"an infant Hercules"

In the Middle Ages — and all previous ages — the rural nature of man dominated the urban. Regional centres like Durham and York had populations of only a few thousand, and significant changes in their street plans, links with other centres, and rivers took place once in a millennium.

This photograph of Middlesbrough shows how dominant the urban nature of man has now become. The industries and employers represented in the photograph provide half the jobs in the County of Cleveland, and a great many of those in nearby counties as well.

The other great change has been the rate of change. In 1828 nothing in the photograph had been built except the hamlet just above the centre — everything else was fields and marshes. Only 50 years later an extenson of the Stockton and Darlington Railway, Old Middlesbrough, and a mass of blast furnaces — called the Ironmasters District — had been completed.

Even the two bridges in the foreground tell a story of rapid change. The Newport Bridge — built in 1934 — was made of steel. The A19 Bridge — built only 44 years later — was made of reinforced concrete.

Middlesbrough

The railways would have enabled the Hartlepools and other east coast ports to handle coal exports without the massive development of the Tees which was carried out by the Tees Navigation Company.

The Stockton and Darlington railway to Port Darlington on the south bank of the Tees was built in 1837. This port was no more of a success than Port Clarence across the river but the Owners of the Middlesbrough Estate bought 500 acres of land in the area and by 1842 had opened Middlesbrough Dock. This dock was built to export coal, but within a few years ironstone was being mined in the Eston Hills and pig iron was being made in the Ironmasters District. Other blast furnaces soon sprang up along the banks of the river, and training walls were constructed to deepen the channel. By 1891 the Tees had become the greatest iron shipping river in the world.

The rest of the area's industrial history is well known, but it needs to be remembered that the great developments on the Tees came about because of stable political conditions and the availability of valuable minerals. The development of Billingham — in its turn — came about because of the availability of salt and anhydrite.

Coal is the only mineral which is still available locally in large quantities — but coal now has its rivals in gas, oil and nuclear power!

Scugdale Jet Mining

Compared to the devastating effect of alum mining on the coastline, jet mining in the 19thC was relatively inconspicuous and serves to remind us of the past working life of the area.

Jet itself is fossilised conifer and is found in a seam of black shale only 25 ft. (8m) thick — which is called Jet Rock.

Old tips can be seen on the hills between Guisborough and Roseberry Topping, and in the north-west area of the North York Moors where pieces of jet can still be found, and can be worked into ornaments quite easily.

The lines of old jet workings stand out clearly in this photograph of Scugdale above Swainby. The mining here was most active between 1850 and 1892 when mining difficulties — and changing fashions — resulted in the importation of an inferior Spanish jet.

Mining at Guisborough

Tradition has it that in Tudor times Sir Thomas Chaloner of Guisborough was riding near his home when he noticed that the soil and plant life resembled that which he had seen near alum mines on the Continent. In 1600 this led to the development of the first alum mine in England at Belman Bank — two miles to the west of the spoil tip in the foreground of the photograph.

However the mining village of Charlton — seen on the road to Birkbrow — was built by a mining engineer called Charlton in the 1850's and his purpose was not to mine alum — but iron ore.

Iron has been made in Cleveland since prehistoric times and, although the earliest known mediaeval forge is in Glaisdale, the Priory of Guisborough is known to have operated bloomeries in 1223.

In the 19thC the great ore field around Guisborough and along the northern flanks of the Cleveland Hills became the main source of ore for the furnaces of Bolckow & Vaughan in Middlesbrough.

By 1860 600,000 tonnes of iron per year were being produced as a result of successful mining operations like this one at Spawood.

The Mandale Cut

The section of the Tees at the top of the photograph was excavated by the Tees Navigation Company of Stockton in 1810. Until then the course of the river had taken a meandering route following the other three sides of the photograph.

Businessmen in Stockton paid £9,800 for the Mandale Cut — and £25,995 for the Portrack Cut — in order to improve their outlet to the sea and to fight off the challenge from the new port of Middlesbrough. The original Portrack section of the river can be seen in the top right hand corner.

One of the results of these cuts was a series of lawsuits on behalf of the owners of the original river frontages and another was the transference of the Mandale swamps from Durham into Yorkshire.

The swamps were later drained and the area was developed into a racecourse.

Roseberry Topping

This landmark for the whole of ancient and modern Cleveland was named Odinsberg — the hill of Odin — by the Anglo-Saxons when they arrived on the Tees estuary, after the departure of the Romans. They named it after their pagan god of wind, tide and movement.

It was here in the late Bronze Age that a smith left his bronze axe heads and tools in a crevice on the far side of the hill. They were found in 1830 and are now in Sheffield Museum.

It seems appropriate that, as a symbol of Cleveland, this hill should have looked down on two iron ages. There are several settlements from the first Iron Age around the hill, and two millennia later in 1880 mining for ore was started by the Roseberry Ironstone Company, which at one time produced over 1000 tonnes of ore per day.

Part of the peak collapsed in 1921 and mining ceased in 1926.

ACKNOWLEDGEMENTS

No author writes a book entirely on his own — especially his first one — and I would like to thank the many people who gave their time to make this a better book.

I would particularly like to thank Blaise Vyner of the Archaeology Section — Cleveland County and Marianne Deans M.A. (Oxon) for commenting on the whole of the manuscript and the latter for helping with the index.

I would also like to thank John Proud, Dr. David Deans Bsc., PhD., Robin Cook M.A. (Oxon), Carol Cook and members of the staff of the Archaeology Section — Cleveland County for commenting on various chapters. I am grateful to the owners of many of the properties photographed for their helpful advice and to members of my family for helping with the index and for making those suggestions which no-one else liked to make.

The Archaeology Section — North Yorkshire kindly made available data from their computerised records of a number of archaeological sites, and the Archives and Libraries of both Cleveland and North Yorkshire allowed me access to their records, maps and reference books. The Yorkshire Archaeological Society and the Teesside Archaeological Society provided invaluable forums for recent archaeological activities.

Finally I would like to thank the Windsports Centre, Wombleton Airfield near Helmsley for keeping my plane in the air, the Cleveland Camera Mart of Middlesbrough for keeping a rather temperamental Bronica EC in working order and Sandra Whiteland for typing the manuscript at least twice, without the benefit of a word processor.

Text Acknowledgements

I would like to thank the authors listed below, for the assistance which their books, pamphlets and articles gave me in the preparation of "Ancient Cleveland — From The Air".

J.C. Atkinson, Rev'd	History of Cleveland — Ancient and Modern (1877)
L. Adkins & R.A. Adkins	The Handbook of British Archaeology
M.W. Beresford & J.K.S. St. Joseph	Mediaeval England — An Aerial Survey
M.W. Beresford M.A.	The Lost Villages of Yorkshire (Yorkshire Archaeological Journal)
ASA Briggs	A Social History of England
W. Breakell	Stone Causeways of the North York Moors
M.M. Brown	Saxon and Viking Cleveland (Archaeology of Cleveland)
M.M. Brown & L. Still	Cleveland History from the Air
C. Bainbridge	North Yorkshire & North Humberside
J.C. Cox LL.D., F.S.A.	The Parish Churches of England (1935)
R. Cartwright	Spout House — The Old Sun Inn
The Department of the Environment	Scarborough Castle
	Helmsley Castle
	Mount Grace Priory
F. & H.W. Elgee	The Archaeology of Yorkshire (1933)
F. Elgee	Early Man in North East Yorkshire (1930)
	The Romans in Cleveland (1923)
J Graves, Rev'd	The History of Cleveland (1808)
P Gilyard — Beer	Guisborough Priory
F. Hewitt, Rev'd (Ed)	The Ancient Crypt Church of St. Mary Lastingham
T. Hinde (Ed)	The Domesday Book
R.H. Hayes & J.G. Rutter	Wade's Causeway
J. Hawkes	The Atlas of Early Man
J. Hurst	Ryedale Folk Museum
J.K. Harrison & J.K. Almond (Eds)	Industrial Archaeology in Cleveland — A Guide
G. Howard	Castle Howard
M.D. Heubner	Ormesby Hall
W. Hornsby & R. Stonton	Huntcliff & Goldsborough Signal Stations
R. Inman	Roman Cleveland (Archaeology of Cleveland)
R. Muir	History from the Air
	The Lost Villages of Britain
A. Mee (Ed)	The Kings England — Yorkshire North Riding
J.S. Owen	Industrial Archaeology in the North Yorkshire Moors — (Industrial Archaeology in Cleveland — A Guide)
J.W. Ord	The History and Antiquities of Cleveland (1846)
C. Platt	Medieval Britain From the Air
A. Phillips M.A. (Oxon)	A look round the Monasteries of North-East Yorkshire
N. Pevsner	Yorkshire — The North Riding
W. Page (Ed)	The Victorian History of the Counties of England (1912)
A. Penn	St. Gregory's Minster, Kirkdale
B.K. Roberts	Village Plans
	Village Plans in County Durham (Mediaeval Archaeology)
A. Raistrick M.Sc., PhD., (Ed)	North York Moors National Park
D.A. Spratt	The Archaeology of Cleveland (Ed)
	Prehistoric & Roman Archaeology in North-East Yorkshire
	The Cleave Dyke System (Yorkshire Archaeological Journal)
D.A. Spratt & I.G. Simmons	Prehistoric Activity & Environment on the North York Moors (Journal of Archaeological Science)
L. Still	Medieval Cleveland (The Archaeology of Cleveland)
L. Still & J. Southeran M.A.	Medieval Origins of Billingham
C. Stanley	The History of Britain — An Aerial View
B.N. Tinkle & D.A. Spratt	Great Ayton Moor Enclosure
P. Turner B.A.	The Church of St. Thomas — Brompton in Allertonshire
M.W. Thompson	Pickering Castle
A.J. Toynbee	A Study of History
B.E. Vyner	Recent Excavations in Cleveland
H. Wade & R. White	Stainsby DMV
F. Whellan (Ed)	The History of Durham (1894)
V. Watts	The History of Place Names In Cleveland
A. Wright	Cleveland — A Pictorial History
R. Woodhouse	Castles in Cleveland
L. Waring	St. Cuthbert's Church — Billingham
S. White M.A. (Cantab) A.C.I.S.	The North York Moors — An Introduction
P.H. Vaughan, Rev'd.	All Saints' Church, Hovingham.

The dates of books — which were first published more than 50 years ago — are shown in brackets after the name of the book.

Picture Acknowledgements

I would particularly like to thank Margaret M. Nairn — my mother-in-law — for her artists impressions of ancient Cleveland at the beginning of the first five chapters on pages 11, 21, 31, 41 and 53.

"History of Cleveland — Ancient and Modern" by J.C. Atkinson, Rev'd.	Group of Urns	p. 21
Archaeology Section, Cleveland County	Photograph of Crown End, Westerdale by L. Still	p. 29
Archaeology Section, Cleveland County	Impression of Thorpe Thewles in 100 BC by A. Hutchinson	p. 37
"The Victorian History of the Counties of England" (1912)	Plan of Topcliffe Castle	p. 67
Footsteps Books — "Stone Causeways of the North York Moors"	Bow Bridge, Castleton	p. 97
"The Anglo-Saxon Chronicles"	Photograph of Durham Cathedral by Walter Scott	p. 85
Archaeology Section, Cleveland County	Photograph of Yarm by B.E. Vyner	p. 101
"The Victorian History of the Counties of England" (1912)	Plan of Whorlton Castle	p. 113
The Ordnance Survey	Map of Great Moorsholme (1853)	p. 121
Trustees of Sir William Turner's Homes	Photograph of the "Hospital"	p. 131
"Industrial Archaeology in Cleveland — A Guide"	Photograph of the Transporter by J.K. Harrison	p. 143
Beamish Museum	Photograph of the Hetton Locomotive	p. 143

This is an index of PROPER NAMES but it **includes** commercial minerals mentioned in the chapter on Industrial Archaeology.
Page numbers in **bold type** refer to photographs and illustrations.

R

S

T

U

V

W

Y

Z